WHAT IS SUSHI?

Sushi is a Japanese cuisine consisting of specially prepared rice and some form of raw or cooked fish or seafood.

Although you may identify the phrase sushi with raw fish, the rice is the most significant component. The sour flavor of the vinegared rice is indeed what the name "sushi" alludes to. Sushi always includes rice, regardless of the toppings or contents.

Sushi rice is so crucial in Japan that sushi chefs must go through years of training merely to learn how to properly prepare the rice before they can handle any fish or seafood.

SUSHI RICE

Sushi rice is a medium-grained white rice that has been seasoned with vinegar and salt and sugar. The most common type of sushi rice is Japonica, namely the Koshihikari cultivar.

Japonica rice has a medium grain size and slightly rounded grains, which distinguishes it from the skinnier, longer-grained rice we're used to in the West, known as indica rice. Japonica rice is more starchy than indica rice, having greater quantities of a starch called amylopectin.

This added starch makes it sticky when cooked, making it easier to chew with chopsticks and great for molding together to produce sushi.

TYPES OF SUSHI

NIGIRI

Despite the fact that all sushi is created using rice, there are only two varieties of sushi: nigiri and maki.

Nigiri sushi is an oval-shaped pile of rice topped with a slice of fish or seafood. The fish or seafood is normally raw, although it can also be fermented or cooked, as in the case of eel or shrimp.

The Japanese term nigiri roughly translates to "grip" in English. As a result, the Japanese name nigiri-zushi roughly translates to "hand-pressed" sushi.

The key is that nigiri sushi is made by hand, with the rice molded by hand and the fish or other topping pushed on top by hand. Between the fish and the rice, the chef may add a dash of wasabi. The rice's stickiness, along with the wetness from the topping, aids in the adhesion of the raw fish strip to the mound of rice beneath.

Tuna, salmon, and yellowtail are common raw fish choices for nigiri sushi. Another popular topping is fatty tuna, which is made from the belly of a bluefin tuna. Minced scallions or ginger can be used as garnishes.

Surprisingly, nigiri sushi is designed to be eaten with your hands rather than chopsticks, despite how you're undoubtedly used to eating it. While dipping the sushi in soy sauce is permissible, the proper method is to flip it over so that the fish side, not the rice side, gets dipped in the sauce. It's considered a serious faux pas to leave rice grains in your soy sauce.

MAKI

Maki, on the other hand, is a style of sushi in which the rice and fish are wrapped in a sheet of nori seaweed. There are a few different varieties of maki.

Maki-zushi is a cylinder-shaped Japanese dish made out of a sheet of dried seaweed called nori folded around a layer of rice and toppings that can include raw fish, cooked seafood, vegetables, and even cream cheese.

After that, the rolled cylinder or tube is divided into bite-sized pieces. When the roll is made from the inside out, it is called ura-maki, which literally means "inside-out roll." The rice is on the exterior of ura-maki, while the seaweed and fillings are on the inside. Maki, like nigiri, is best eaten with your hands.

Thin rolls, known as hoso-maki, and thick rolls, known as futo-maki, are two types of maki-zushi.

There's also a maki variation called gunkan-maki, which is also known as "battleship rolls" due to its battleship-like form. They're a hybrid between nigiri and maki in that they have a hand-molded rice foundation with a nori strip around it that acts as a receptacle for toppings that won't stay on by themselves, including fish roe, finely chopped raw fish, or vegetables like sweet corn kernels in a mayonnaise dressing.

UNI SUSHI

We have one of the most peculiar varieties of sushi, uni sushi, under the category of gunkan-maki. Uni refers to a sea urchin's sex organs. It has a sweet flavor and a little sticky consistency and is shaped like tongues.

This style of sushi may be fairly pricey due to the intensive effort needed in harvesting the uni. However, for those who enjoy it, it is well worth the money. The most important aspect of uni is that it should be solid and dry. It's probably not fresh if it appears damp.

TEMAKI SUSHI

Finally, we have temaki, or hand rolls, in which the nori is rolled loosely into a cone-like form with the fillings within, similar to a huge ice-cream cone, rather than securely wrapped around the rice and fillings.

1.SANDWICH SUSHI ROLLS

Total Time: 10 minutes | **Yield:** 12

INGREDIENTS

❖ Tip Top Supersoft High Fiber White Toast, 4 slices

Tuna Mayo

❖ 95g canned tuna
❖ 2 Tbsp mayonnaise
❖ ¼ cucumber, finely sliced

Ham and Cheese

❖ 4 ham slices
❖ 30g grated cheese
❖ 2 lettuce leaves, or

Chicken avo

❖ 75g cooked chicken breast, sliced
❖ 1 small avocado, finely sliced
❖ ½ capsicum, finely sliced

INSTRUCTIONS

1. Remove the bread's crust and give it a gentle roll with a rolling pin. Using margarine or butter, apply it to the edges.
2. Mix mayonnaise and tuna in a bowl and spread on toast for a tasty sandwich. Slices of cucumber should be added, and then the bread should be rolled up, leaving a 2cm gap in the middle.

3. A slice of ham, some grated cheese, and a half-leaf of lettuce are all that's needed to make this sandwich. Make three rounds out of each sandwich.
4. Roll up the chicken, avocado, and capsicum in the tortillas to make chicken avo. Slice each sandwich into three equal halves.
5. Wrap each piece in plastic and store in an airtight container. Wait until ready to serve or put into lunchboxes before storing in the fridge.

2.SPICY JACKFRUIT SUSHI

Total Time: 30 minutes | **Yield:** 8

INGREDIENTS

For the spicy jackfruit

- ❖ 1 can young jackfruit, in brine
- ❖ 1 tbsp tamari or gluten-free soy sauce
- ❖ 2 1/2 tsp Sriracha, divided
- ❖ 2 tbsp nutritional yeast
- ❖ *Store-bought or homemade vegan mayo*: 1/4 cup
- ❖ 1 1/2 tsp sesame oil

To assemble the sushi rolls

- ❖ 4 sheets of nori
- ❖ 2 cups prepared sushi rice**
- ❖ 1 avocado, sliced
- ❖ 1/2 cup gluten-free rice crispies

INSTRUCTIONS

For the spicy jackfruit

1. Delete the core from the jackfruit pieces and rinse well, breaking up the jackfruit so it is stringy.
2. In a saucepan, cover the jackfruit with water. Add in the tamari, 1 tsp of sriracha, and nutritional yeast.
3. Simmer the jackfruit for 15-20 minutes.
4. Remove from heat and rinse the jackfruit. Squeeze out excess liquid.

5. Mix the jackfruit, mayo, 1 1/2 tsp of sriracha, and the sesame oil together in a bowl. Refrigerate until ready to use.

To assemble the rolls

1. Check out some sushi-making tutorials on YouTube if you've never done it before!
2. Spread 1/2 cup of cooked sushi rice over the nori on the sushi mat. Stack a quarter-cup of spicy jackfruit, a quarter-cup of sliced avocado, and two tablespoons of rice crispies horizontally, near to the nori's bottom edge.
3. Roll out the sushi. If necessary, add a little water to assist the seaweed's edge stay.
4. Slice the sushi roll into eight equal pieces. " I usually eat the ends to "test" the dish since they never look good.
5. To serve, top with wasabi and ginger. If desired, add extra rice crispies to the rolls.

3.GOLDEN BEETS NIRIGI SUSHI

Total Time: 1 hour 15 minute | **Servings :** 2 people

INGREDIENTS

- ❖ 3 oz golden beets (estimate 0.5 oz per beet slice, 3 sushis per person)
- ❖ 6 oz cooked brown rice (or use sticky sushi rice for a stickier variety)
- ❖ soy sauce to taste
- ❖ wasabi to taste
- ❖ greens (for decoration; baby kale, lettuce, parsley)

INSTRUCTIONS

1. Prepare the brown rice in advance. For a stickier version, use sushi rice or add a tiny amount of oil or butter to the rice before cooking to help brown rice get stickier once cold. Then let it cool down in the fridge for at least one hour.
2. Prepare also the beets in advance. You can use golden beets for a yellow to orange color, or cook and store them with red beets, letting the colors blend more as we did for this recipe.
3. Estimating one ounce of rice, make a nigiri rice ball by pressing firmly the rice grains together several times then setting them on a plate. Put 3 nigiri balls per plate per person or adjust to preference.
4. Slice the golden beet to match the size of sushi and place the beets bits on top.
5. Add soy sauce and wasabi to taste, as well as greens on the side for decoration. Tasty and fresh greens can of course be eaten and enjoyed with the vegan nigiri sushi.

4.PEANUT TOFU SUSHI

Preparation: 60 Min | **Cooking:** 20 Min | **Makes:** 5-6 Rolls

INGREDIENTS

SUSHI

- ❖ 450 g / 2 cups sushi rice
- ❖ 1 tsp fine sea salt
- ❖ 5-6 nori sheets

FILLING

- ❖ 10 radishes, pickled (see METHOD) or raw
- ❖ In the case of radishes, you'll need to add another 60 ml (about 14 cup) of rice wine vinegar to the mix. juice of limes
- ❖ ½ tsp fine sea salt
- ❖ 2 tbsp maple syrup (plus 2 tbsp of pickling radishes)
- ❖ 200 g / 7 oz firm tofu, pressed
- ❖ 3 tbsp tamari (for GF version) or soy sauce, plus more to serve
- ❖ 60 g / ¼ cup 100% natural* peanut butter (smooth or crunchy)
- ❖ 1 tbsp toasted sesame oil (optional)
- ❖ a small garlic clove, finely grated
- ❖ ½-1 tsp Chinese five-spice, adjust to taste
- ❖ 1 long cucumber, cored and julienned
- ❖ 1-2 spring onions / scallions, cut into thin strips lengthwise
- ❖ 30 g / ¼ cup toasted peanuts, chopped roughly (optional)

METHOD

RICE

1. Make several passes through the water with the sushi rice to remove any remaining impurities.
2. Cover 480 ml / 2 cups of water with washed rice in a big saucepan with a glass lid. Slowly bring the mixture to a boil by covering it with a lid. As soon as the water is boiling, reduce the heat to a low setting and let the rice to simmer before it has absorbed all the liquid. Ten more minutes after the water has been absorbed, leave it covered on a warm stove for the final 10 minutes of cooking.
3. Add salt to the cooked rice in a big Pyrex-style dish by folding the salt in with a spatula (avoiding crushing the grains). Once it's cooled, remove the rice from the pan.
4. QUICK-PICKLED RADISHES (optional)
5. Place thinly sliced radishes in a clean container or bowl.
6. Combine 60 ml/14 cups of water and rice wine vinegar in a small saucepan. For milder pickles, add 12 tsp of salt and 2 tbsp of maple syrup. Bring the mixture to a simmer.
7. Set aside the pickling liquid after pouring it over the radishes.

PEANUT TOFU

1. Make long (about 0.75 cm / 0.3″ thick) batons out of tofu. Using 112 tbsp of soy sauce, coat the fish in the shallow dish. Cook at a temperature of 190 C/375 F while the marinade is marinating.
2. Combine the peanut butter, 112 tbsp tamari/soy sauce, maple syrup, rice wine vinegar/lime juice, sesame oil,

grated garlic, and Chinese five-spice in a bowl. Stir well. Set away for later.

3. Bake the tofu batons for about 10 minutes on a baking sheet lined with parchment paper.

4. Tofu should be coated with about half of the peanut glaze and baked for another 10 minutes.

ASSEMBLY

1. Be prepared with a small container of water. A sushi mat or tightly folded kitchen towel can be used as an alternative to a sushi mat. The glossy side of a nori sheet should face up. To seal, leave a 1 cm / 0.4″ margin at the very top of the nori sheet after spreading the rice evenly. Continue pushing the rice into the mat as you spread it out evenly. This will help keep the roll tightly rolled.

2. Start by placing radish halves, cucumber sticks, and shredded spring onion along the bottom edge of the nori sheet, leaving some space below so that you can fold the nori sheet over the filling. Continue by adding baked tofu, more drizzles of sauce, and crushed toasted peanuts (if using).

3. Squeeze hard with both hands while gently rolling the roll on the mat. Make it a habit to come back and double-check that everything is still in place.

4. The next step is to brush water on the edge of the roll with your finger in order to seal it. Once you've completed rolling it up, place it somewhere safe. The leftover nori sheets must be used to complete the final four processes.

5. Using a sharp knife, slice the sushi rolls into 1 cm (0.4″) slices. Tomato sauce, soy sauce, and watered down peanuts are all that's needed to make this dish complete.

5.CURRIED MILLET SUSHI

Prep-Time: 25 Minute | **Ready In:** 45 Minutes | **Makes:** 4 Rolls

INGREDIENTS

- ❖ 1 cup millet
- ❖ 1½ teaspoons curry powder
- ❖ 1½ teaspoons onion powder
- ❖ 1½ teaspoons garlic powder
- ❖ ¼ cup brown rice vinegar
- ❖ 2 tablespoons pure maple syrup
- ❖ 1½ teaspoons arrowroot powder
- ❖ ¼ teaspoon sea salt
- ❖ 4 toasted nori sheets
- ❖ 1 medium sweet red pepper, cut into eighteen 4×¼-inch strips
- ❖ 1 cup carrots, finely shredded
- ❖ 2 small avocados, thinly sliced
- ❖ 1 cup fresh spinach
- ❖ Low-sodium tamari
- ❖ Wasabi paste

INSTRUCTIONS

1. Combine the millet, curry, onion, and garlic powders, and 2 cups of water in a skillet over medium-high heat. Simmer after boiling. Cozy 20 minutes. Remove food from heat.
2. Pour vinegar, maple syrup, arrowroot powder, and salt into a small basin and mix well. Stir the heated millet into the mixture. Let the pan sit covered for 10 mins.
3. Set up a work area where the rolls may be assembled. Once the nori sheet has been put out on the cutting board,

place it lengthwise on the sushi mat. The millet should be spooned onto the nori. Millet should be pressed into an equal layer on top and bottom of nori, leaving a 1-inch border around the sides. Over the millet, arrange one-fourth of the vegetable strips, the avocado slices, and the spinach in long, long rows.

4. Nori sheets may be rolled over your vegetables, but take care to tuck them under as you go so that they don't get pushed out of the top. Press the nori edge into the roll to seal it. Seal the edge with water if necessary.

5. Cut the roll in half by dipping a long, sharp knife in water. Make eight pieces by halving each piece twice and then halving it a third time.

6. In order to manufacture and cut three additional rolls, repeat Steps 3 through 5. With tamari and wasabi paste, serve the sushi rolls as an appetizer.

6. SPICY SALMON AND AVOCADO CAULIFLOWER RICE SUSHI ROLL

Total Time: 20 minutes | **Yield**: 3-4 rolls

INGREDIENTS

Cauliflower Rice:

- ❖ 3 cups grated cauliflower rice
- ❖ 2 Tablespoons rice vinegar
- ❖ 2 teaspoons tapioca starch
- ❖ pinch of salt

Sushi Roll:

- ❖ 1/2 lb sushi-grade salmon (or tuna or smoked salmon)
- ❖ 1/2 teaspoon Frank's Red Hot (use siracha instead if Whole30/Paleo isn't a concern)
- ❖ 1 large avocado, sliced
- ❖ 1 cup cilantro
- ❖ 1/2 cucumber cut into small "sticks"
- ❖ 3–4 sheets of nori
- ❖ (A bamboo sushi roller is also needed.)

Dipping Sauce:

- ❖ Coco amino and a little bit of red pepper flakes
- ❖ Spicy Mayo (optional):
- ❖ 3/4 cup Compliant mayo
- ❖ 1–2 teaspoons Frank's Red Hot or Siracha (not Whole30) – (mix per your desired spicy level)

INSTRUCTIONS

1. grate the cauliflower (I would HIGHLY recommend grating it so that it is the right texture)
2. Grate cauliflower and cook it on medium.
3. Using a wooden spoon, stir the cauliflower for 3 minutes.
4. Rice vinegar and a dash of salt complete the dish.
5. The vinegar should coat the cauliflower in approximately 2 minutes, so keep stirring.
6. Stir in the tapioca starch until smooth.
7. Remove the rice from the heat and place it in a separate bowl to cool.
8. Place a paper towel on a big platter.
9. Add a paper towel on top of the rice and push down to absorb any extra moisture.
10. Refill the bowl with the cauliflower rice.
11. Cut the salmon into cubes and set them in a serving basin.
12. Franks Red Hot or Siracha can be added and stirred in to coat; leave away.
13. Cutting board: Place a bamboo sushi roller on the cutting board.
14. Add a sheet of nori on top of it.
15. Using the back of a metal spoon, press down on the cauliflower rice to spread it out and create a thin, compacted layer on the nori.
16. Work your way up the nori sheet, away from your body, leaving about an inch of the nori sheet exposed with rice at the top.
17. Lay down the cucumber, cilantro, salmon, and avocado in a straight line, parallel to the nori sheet's bottom and about an inch from the edge. Repeat with the other ingredients.

18. To fold over the fish, etc., raise up the bottom of the nori sheet closest to you, tucking the nori sheet under, and then continue dragging the bamboo roller away from your body while you press down hard on the roll as you go. Then, fold the nori sheet over the salmon, etc.
19. Once you've finished rolling, keep pulling away from yourself.
20. Use a razor-sharp knife to cut 1 inch slices, cleaning the blade clean after each cut.
21. Coco aminos should be added right away.
22. Garnish with more cilantro, black sesame seeds, and spicy mayo.

7.TUNA AND CORN SUSHI SHIPS

Prep: 50 minutes | **Cook:** 15 minutes | **Makes:** 18

INGREDIENTS

Basic sushi rice

- ❖ 1 cup sushi rice
- ❖ 1/4 cup Obento mirin seasoning

Filling

- ❖ 185g can tuna in springwater, drained, flaked
- ❖ 125g can corn kernels, drained, rinsed
- ❖ 1 1/2 tbsp whole-egg mayonnaise
- ❖ 1 tbsp finely chopped fresh garlic chives (see note)
- ❖ 3 nori sheets
- ❖ Finely chopped fresh garlic chives, to serve

INSTRUCTIONS

1. Make the sushi rice as follows: Rinse and drain the rice three times, or until the water is completely clear. Set up a sieve with a bowl of rice inside. Allow to sit for 10 minutes to allow the water to evaporate.

2. 1 cup cold water and 1 cup cooked rice should be combined in a small saucepan. A small pot should be filled with one cup of cold water and one cup of cooked rice. Cover. Begin heating. Reduce the temperature. Using a cover, cook for 12 minutes or until all the liquid has been absorbed. Removing the food from the heat is necessary. For ten minutes, keep your head and shoulders covered.

3. Transfer the rice to a ceramic dish large enough to hold it. Stir the rice to break up any lumps with a spatula. As the rice cools, add the spice in a slow, steady stream, raising and turning it constantly.

4. In a medium bowl, combine tuna, corn, mayonnaise, and chives. Mix thoroughly. Make six equal strips from one side of the nori sheets.

5. Fill a small basin with ice-cold water Get some water on your fingertips, then shake off the excess. At a time, form a rectangle of rice with gently rounded sides using 1 spoonful of the rice mixture. Seal the nori around the rice, and then trim away any extra.

6. Add tuna salad to the top of the rice. Extra chives can be added to the dish before serving.

8.ASPARAGUS SMOKED SALMON SUSHI

Total Time: 30 minutes | **Yield:** 4 Rolls

INGREDIENTS

- ❖ Several spears of asparagus
- ❖ Sesame oil
- ❖ Soy sauce
- ❖ Cooked sushi rice (recipe here)
- ❖ Nori or soy sushi wrappers
- ❖ Smoked salmon
- ❖ Greek cream cheese (or Neufchatel)
- ❖ Sriracha sauce
- ❖ Chopped green onion
- ❖ Black sesame seeds (or white ... or chia seeds)

INSTRUCTIONS

1. Set the temperature of the oven to 400 degrees Fahrenheit. A teaspoon of sesame oil should be drizzled over the asparagus spears before baking, and the spears should be gently tossed to distribute the oil evenly. Over the asparagus, drizzle a little soy sauce. Toss the asparagus in the oven for approximately 10 to 15 minutes, or until the spears are just beginning to brown.

2. If you have a bamboo or silicone baking mat, place a sheet of nori shining side down on top of it. Sushi rice should be used to thoroughly cover the nori. Keep the rice from sticking to your fingers by dipping them in water. Make a thin layer of rice on top of the nori by pressing it down. After you've re-wetted your hands, dab some water over the rice on top. Make sure the nori is on top before adding sesame seeds.

3. A third of the way down the nori sheet, make a stripe of fillings. I started with a thin layer of cream cheese, followed by a thin layer of sriracha and a thin layer of smoked salmon. Green onion can be sprinkled on the stripe. When making a "inside-out" sushi, you may use more filling because the nori is on the outside of the roll.

4. After folding the nori/rice sheet over the toppings and pressing towards you, begin rolling the sushi. Once you've rolled up the first half, continue to roll the sushi, pressing to form a cylinder shape. If there are any "gaps" in the middle of the sushi roll after you've finished it, press down a bit harder.

5. Cut the sushi into 1/2- 3/4-inch thick slices using a very sharp, moist knife. If necessary, repeat. Offer wasabi, pickled ginger and additional sriracha to those who want it spicy.

9. AVOCADO SAUERKRAUT SUSHI RECIPE

Total: 20 minutes | **Serving:** 1 roll

INGREDIENTS

- ❖ 2 Nori sheets
- ❖ 1 cup cooked sushi rice
- ❖ 1 T. seasoned rice wine vinegar
- ❖ 1 Avocado, mashed or use guacamole
- ❖ 1 cup Sauerkraut, drained (store-bought or homemade)
- ❖ 1/2 Cucumber
- ❖ 1/2 Carrot
- ❖ 1/4 cup Daikon Radish

Fresh sprouts (optional)

- ❖ ½ teaspoon of both Ginger and Garlic mashed
- ❖ Sesame Seeds, toasted
- ❖ Umeboshi Plum Paste, optional
- ❖ Wasabi Paste, optional

INSTRUCTIONS

1. Take time to chill down the sushi rice the day or many hours before creating the sushi. Once the rice has cooled, add rice vinegar to it.
2. Slice or julienne all of the veggies and combine with the minced garlic and ginger.
3. Make a paste out of the avocado.
4. Fill a small basin halfway with hot water and use it to create the sushi rolls.
5. Set the nori on a flexible surface, such as a bamboo sushi mat or a tea towel coated with plastic wrap before assembling the sushi.

6. To begin, lay down the nori sheet with the glossy side facing down and the horizontal lines running along it.
7. Spread rice over nori, leaving 12 inches of nori as a border.
8. On top of it, spread the avocado mash.
9. Next, add the veggies and sauerkraut.
10. It is best to apply a modest quantity of Umeboshi and Wasabi paste.
11. A hard roll may be made by squeezing the nori strongly from the bottom.
12. The nori will stick better if you dab a little water on top of it before rolling it up.
13. Use a very sharp knife to make six equal pieces when cutting across (dipped in water to reduce friction).
14. Add sesame seeds to finish!

10.SUSHI RICE WITH APPLE, PEPPERS AND WATERCRESS

Total Time: 15 min | **Serving:** 8 pieces

INGREDIENTS

- ❖ ½yellow bell pepper
- ❖ 2 bowlscress
- ❖ 1smaller apple (red)
- ❖ 50 grams cream cheese
- ❖ 1 tbsp lemon juice
- ❖ 1 generous pinchhorseradish (from a jar)
- ❖ salt
- ❖ white peppers
- ❖ 200 gramsfinished sushi rice
- ❖ vinegar water (for hands)
- ❖ 4roasted nori seaweed

PREPARATION

1. Rinse and slice the pepper. The watercress should be well cleaned and dried using a salad spinner. The apple should be rinsed, cored, and quartered before being cut into pieces. Lemon juice, horseradish, salt, and pepper can all be added to the cream cheese mixture.

2. Make 8 servings of the sushi rice. Each part should be formed into an elongated shape using water and vinegar on your hands. To divide the seaweed sheets, cut them in half along their length. Place a rice portion on top of a sheet with the smooth side down and brush the top with a little cream cheese. Assemble your ingredients and fry the roll as a unit while pressing down firmly to ensure it holds its shape.

11.VEGAN AVOCADO & ROASTED RED PEPPER SUSHI

Total Time: 40 minutes | **Yield:** 4 sushi rolls

INGREDIENTS

Sushi Rice

- ❖ 1 1/2 cups filtered water
- ❖ 1 cup organic white sushi rice (or 1 cup washed brown rice)
- ❖ 2 TBSP organic brown rice vinegar
- ❖ 1 TBSP organic coconut sugar
- ❖ pinch of sea salt

Sushi

- ❖ 4 sheets sushi nori (dried seaweed)
- ❖ 1 roasted red bell pepper (thinly sliced)
- ❖ 2 avocados, thinly sliced
- ❖ handful of sprouts (optional)

For serving

- ❖ Tamari
- ❖ pickled ginger
- ❖ sesame seeds
- ❖ wasabi

INSTRUCTIONS

1. In a pot, boil sushi rice and water. Place a lid and turn the heat down to simmer. Cook for 20 minutes or until the rice is cooked and the water has been absorbed. Delete

the pot from the heat and let it sit for another 10 minutes with the lid on.

2. Stir regularly while heating the vinegar, coconut sugar, and sea salt in a small saucepan on medium until the sugar and salt are completely dissolved. Take a break and let the mixture cool down.

3. Stir in the vinegar mixture when it has cooled to ensure that the rice is well-coated. Keep the sushi rice in the fridge until you're ready to make it.

4. To assemble, thinly slice the avocado and the roasted red peppers.

5. Your sushi is ready to be made. The glossy side of the nori sheet should face down on your sushi mat. A thin coating of rice should be patted onto the nori using your hands bathed in water (to avoid sticking).

6. This is where you'll add some flavor to the bottom half of the rice by layering half an avocado, some strips of roasted red pepper, and optional sprouts in a horizontal line (see photo).

7. Once the rice and nori have been rolled over the vegetables, turn the mat over to compress and form the roll. Once you've rolled it all up, repeat the process. Seal the roll by dabbing some water on the outer border. Using a sushi knife, slice the roll into eight pieces. Once all rice and filling is used up, make another three or four sushi rolls, depending on how much you load each one. Sushi is best eaten fresh, although leftovers can be stored in the refrigerator for up to two days.

12. CUCUMBER AVOCADO SUSHI ROLLS

Total Time: 15 Mins | **Servings:** 2

INGREDIENTS

- ❖ 1 English cucumber
- ❖ 1 avocado mashed
- ❖ 1/2 lemon juiced
- ❖ 1/4 cup fresh mint and basil rough chopped
- ❖ 2 tbsp hemp seeds
- ❖ salt and pepper to taste

INSTRUCTIONS

1. Make long, thin slices out of the cucumber using a vegetable peeler.
2. Add the salt, pepper, and lemon juice to the mashed avocado in a bowl and mix well.
3. A thin coating of avocado should be spread on one end of a cucumber strip, and then the other end.
4. Roll up and decorate with hemp seeds and fresh herbs.
5. Keep going and have fun.

13.SAVOY CABBAGE WITH RICE AND MUSHROOM STUFFING

Total Time: 1 Hr 10 Min | **Serves For:** 4

INGREDIENTS

- ❖ Rice Vinegar 250 g, sushi
- ❖ Cabbage 4 - 5 large leaves
- ❖ Sesame Oil 1 tbsp
- ❖ Mushrooms 250 g, mixed (shiitake, chestnut, chopped)
- ❖ Ginger thumb-size piece, finely chopped
- ❖ Garlic 1 clove, finely chopped
- ❖ Soy Sauce 1 - 2 tbsp light
- ❖ Lime juice 1 - 2 tbsp
- ❖ Rice Vinegar 2 tbsp
- ❖ Sugar 1 tbsp
- ❖ Salt 1/2 tsp
- ❖ Wasabi 2 tsp
- ❖ Chives 12

PREPARATION

1. In a sieve, place the sushi rice and swish it around until the water runs clear.
2. In a pan, cover with water and drain for a few seconds before re-filling the pan if necessary.
3. A boil should be reached before being reduced to simmer for 20-25 minutes, or until the rice is done.
4. Set aside, covered.
5. Boil the savoy cabbage leaves for 1 minute in boiling water.
6. Pat dry after rinsing with cold water.

7. Sesame oil should be heated in a pan before using. Cook the mushrooms, ginger, and garlic in a gentle, oven-safe sauce until soft.
8. Set aside the light soy sauce and lime juice after stirring them in together in a small bowl.
9. Vinegar and salt should be mixed thoroughly before adding sugar.
10. Using a fork, gently incorporate the cooked rice into the mixture.
11. Place the cabbage leaves on a big sheet of foil or cling film, gently overlapping each other.
12. The lower part of the cabbage leaves should be coated in wasabi.
13. Use your hands to spread the cooked rice over the bottom quarter of each cabbage leaf, followed by a layer of mushrooms.
14. Using the cling film, roll the cabbage leaves into a tight bundle.
15. Cut into 2-inch-long segments, each measuring 4 centimeters in length. Chive stalks can be used to secure each roll.

14. SPICY TOMATO SUSHI ROLLS

Ready In: 1 Hour | **Makes:** 4 Rolls

INGREDIENTS

- ❖ 1½ cups low-sodium vegetable broth
- ❖ ¾ cup dry short grain brown rice
- ❖ 1½ cups frozen riced butternut squash
- ❖ 4 seeded and sliced Roma tomatoes (2 cups)
- ❖ 1 tablespoon tamari (low-sodium)
- ❖ 1 teaspoon grated fresh ginger
- ❖ 1 tablespoon sriracha sauce
- ❖ 2 teaspoons tahini
- ❖ 2 tablespoons rice vinegar (brown)
- ❖ 1 tablespoon maple syrup (pure)
- ❖ 4 8-inch toasted nori sheets
- ❖ ½ of a medium avocado, peeled and sliced
- ❖ 1 Persian cucumber, seeded and sliced into ¼-inch strips lengthwise (5½ oz.)
- ❖ 2 carrots, coarsely shredded (1 cup)
- ❖ 4 scallions (green onions), sliced lengthwise into strips after trimming to 6 inches

INSTRUCTIONS

1. Bring a small saucepan of broth to a rolling boil. Reduce the heat and add the rice, if necessary. Simmer for about 40 minutes, or before the liquid has been absorbed. Cover and cook. Squash and riced butternut squash can be added. Allow for a minimum of five minutes to pass.
2. Meanwhile, combine the following five ingredients for the spicy tomatoes in a dish (through tahini).
3. Mix brown rice with rice vinegar and maple syrup.

4. Place a nori sheet lengthwise on the sushi mat that has been laid out on a cutting board. Spread one-fourth of the rice mixture over the bottom two-thirds of the nori, leaving a 14-inch border on the side borders with moist fingertips. Assemble the other ingredients and place one-fourth on each side of the rice layer. Using a sushi mat, raise and tightly roll the nori toward the unfilled edge. The empty portion of the roll should be brushed with water before being pressed over the top. Make another four rolls using the remaining ingredients. Slice each roll into 1-inch pieces to serve.

15.VEGAN SUMMER ROLLS

Total Time: 20 Mins | **Servings:** 4

INGREDIENTS

- ❖ 8 sheets rice paper
- ❖ 1 cup rice noodles cooked
- ❖ 1 cup lettuce shredded
- ❖ 1 cup carrots julienned
- ❖ 1 cup cucumber julienned
- ❖ 1 cup red cabbage shredded
- ❖ 1 cup cilantro
- ❖ ½ cup mango thinly sliced
- ❖ Peanut Sauce
- ❖ ½ cup peanut butter
- ❖ ¼ cup soy sauce
- ❖ ½ tbsp ginger freshly grated
- ❖ 1 clove garlic minced
- ❖ 1 tbsp sesame oil

- ❖ 1 tsp maple syrup
- ❖ ½ tsp crushed red pepper
- ❖ 3 tbsp cool water

INSTRUCTIONS

1. All ingredients should be cleaned and prepared according to the directions indicated above.
2. Set aside the peanut sauce after combining all of the ingredients.
3. Using a piece of rice paper, soak it entirely in a large bowl of water. As soon as you've finished, remove the noodles from the water and pat them dry with a clean dish towel.
4. Assemble the ingredients in the center of the rice paper and set it on a cutting board (see picture above).
5. As a final step, you will roll the rice paper into a burrito. Pull the side closest to your body over the mound of components, starting at the bottom. When you're finished, tuck the right and left sides under. As a last step, keep rolling up the rice paper (again, picture wrapping up a burrito).
6. Fill and wrap one summer roll at a time, one at a time, until all of the rolls have been completed. Slice in half and serve with the peanut sauce.

16. NORI SUSHI ROLL

Prep: 5 minute | **Cook:** 1 hour | **Servings:** 3 Rolls

INGREDIENTS

For sushi rice

- ❖ 1 cup sushi rice Japanese short-grain rice
- ❖ 1 cup water
- ❖ 1 ½ tablespoon sushi vinegar or a combination of both 1 teaspoon of salt and 2 tablespoons of rice vinegar

Nori sushi rolls:

- ❖ Avocado, cucumber, or roasted sweet potatoes are examples of fillings (other fillings options include shrimp, salmon, pickled vegetables etc.)
- ❖ 3 sheets nori seaweed

METHOD

Make the sushi rice

1. Cold water should be used to wash the rice until the water is clear. In the rice cooker, combine it with the water. The manufacturer's instructions should be followed.
2. Set the rice aside in a big mixing basin to cool down a bit. While the sauce is still hot, add the sushi vinegar and combine well (the mixture of rice vinegar, sugar, and salt).

Make nori sushi rolls

1. If desired, place a plastic wrap sheet on top of the bamboo mat before it is laid out (this will make clean up easier).
2. Remove about a third of the seaweed. Place the remaining nori sheet on top of the bamboo, shiny side down.
3. Spread 3/4 cup of cooked rice evenly over nori, leaving a 1/2-inch gap at the top of the sheet of nori for the topping. Immerse your palm in Tezu vinegar water* to avoid sticking.
4. The contents should be layered on top of rice.
5. With your thumbs, lift the bamboo mat's edge up and over the filling.
6. Press the rice and contents together as you roll the bamboo mat away from you.

17. CRUNCHY ROLL RECIPE

Prep Time: 15 minute | **Cook Time:** 45 minute | **Servings:** 3 rolls

EQUIPMENT

- ❖ Bamboo Sushi Mat
- ❖ Plastic Wrap
- ❖ Ingredients

For the Sushi Rice

- ❖ 1 ½ cup sushi rice
- ❖ 1 ½ cup water
- ❖ 2 tablespoons optional sushi vinegar (or mixing 1 tablespoon of rice vinegar and 1/2 tablespoon of sugar)

For the Tempura California Roll

- ❖ 8 pre-cooked shrimp tempura (you can sub cooked shrimp or imitation crab)
- ❖ a single avocado (ripe but still firm, cut into thin slices. you can sub sliced cucumber)
- ❖ 2 sheets nori (seaweed sheet)

For the Crunchy Topping

- ❖ 1 cup Panko breadcrumbs
- ❖ 2 teaspoons olive oil

Optional for Serving

- ❖ unagi sauce
- ❖ mayo

METHOD

1. Prepare the Sushi Rice and the Other Components
2. A rice cooker should be used to cook the sushi rice after it has been rinsed. Delete from the heat and transfer to a large mixing bowl to cool somewhat. The vinegar can be added while the dish is still hot, so be careful not to overwork it.
3. Cook the shrimp in a tempura style. Shrimp tempura that has been frozen should be baked for 10-15 minutes at 450 degrees F, depending on the shrimp's weight.

Make the Crunchy Topping

1. Large pan, medium heat olive oil
2. . Medium-heat olive oil in a big skillet. Add the panko bread crumbs to the rest of the ingredients and mix well.
3. The panko should be golden brown after only a few minutes of cooking. Stirring up a storm
4. Allow the toasted panko to cool down.

Make Tempera California Rolls

1. Wrap the bamboo mat with plastic wrap (to prevent the rice from sticking to the bamboo).
2. The nori sheet should be cut in half using scissors.
3. Shiny side down, lay half of the nori sheet on top of the bamboo mat.
4. Using a nori sheet, put out about 3/4 cup of cooked rice. Get your hands sprayed with vinegar or Tezu water* before touching the rice. You won't get stuck if you do this.
5. The rice should now be on the bottom of the dish.
6. Place 2-3 pieces of shrimp tempura and two slices of avocado on top of the nori.

7. With your thumbs, lift the bamboo mat's edge up and over the filling.
8. To tighten the bamboo mat, roll it away from you and apply pressure. To finish rolling, bring the two ends together so that they contact.
9. Remove the sandwich's plastic wrapper..

Assemble the Roll

1. Stir in the bread crumb mixture before eating. Replace the plastic wrap on top of the sushi mat. Using your hands, gently squeeze the breadcrumbs together to form a crust around the roll.
2. Remove the mat from the roll using the plastic wrap, but keep the mat itself. The roll is then sliced into bite-sized pieces. Remove the food's plastic wrap. Unagi sauce or mayo are great additions to your meal!

18.BOSTON ROLL

Prep Time: 10 minutes | **Cook Time:** 50 mins | **Servings:** 4 rolls

INGREDIENTS

For Sushi Rice

- ❖ 1 cup sushi rice short-grain sushi rice
- ❖ 1 cup water
- ❖ 1 ½ tablespoons sushi vinegar (optional) or mixing 1 tablespoons rice vinegar, 1/2 tablespoon sugar, and 1/2 teaspoon salt

For Boston Sushi

- ❖ 3-6 tablespoons tobiko (or masago)
- ❖ 6 oz shrimp
- ❖ 1/2 cucumber cut into ½-inch strips
- ❖ 2 sheets nori seaweed sheet
- ❖ 2 avocado ripe but still firm

Optional for Serving:

- ❖ soy sauce
- ❖ wasabi paste

METHOD

1. Rice cooker instructions: Rinse the rice and add water, according to the manufacturer's directions. Put everything in a large dish and refrigerate it. Add sushi vinegar (or rice vinegar, sugar, and salt)
2. to heated sauce and combine well.
3. Before adding the shrimp to the boiling water, season it with a pinch of salt. Cover the shrimp with a lid after

removing the skillet from the heat. Allow the shrimp to rest for 3 to 5 minutes, or until they are fully cooked. Add the shrimp in a bowl of ice water to stop the frying process. Peel the shrimp and discard the tails.

4. Add a bamboo mat on a level surface and cover it with plastic wrap to produce a Boston Sushi Roll (this will make clean up easier and prevent rice from sticking to the bamboo).

5. Cut the nori sheets in thirds once they have been cut in half along the long axis.

6. Once you've started at the edges, work your way in from the middle of the mat.

7. Using a little water, moisten about 3/4 cup of the cooked rice. In the event that lubrication is required, vinegar water can be utilized. The outside of the pan should be coated with a thin, even layer of rice. Applying too much pressure can result in soggy rice.

8. Place the rice and nori on top of each other, with the rice on the bottom, and then switch positions.

9. Shrimp, avocado, and cucumber are placed on top of the nori. Make sure you don't overfill the roll when manufacturing it, otherwise it won't seal properly.

10. To accomplish this, place your thumbs behind the bamboo pad and raise it up and over your teeth.

11. Rolling the mat away from you and applying pressure to the edges can help you tighten the bamboo mat. If you want to finish rolling, do so until the ends meet.

12. After removing the bamboo mat, use a tobiko spreader to cover the top of the roll with tobiko.

13. On top of the plastic wrap, place the sushi mat. Wrap the tobiko securely around the roll using a small amount of pressure.

14. Keep the bamboo mat and the plastic wrap in their original locations. Slice the roll into eight equal pieces with a bread knife. Discard the plastic wrapping from all of the food you've purchased. Enjoy your meal when it's been served!

19.UNAGI SUSHI RECIPE

Prep Time: 10 minute | **Cook Time:** 50 minute | **Servings:** 3 rolls

EQUIPMENT

❖ Bamboo Sushi Mat
❖ Plastic Wrap

INGREDIENTS

For Sushi Rice

❖ 1 cup sushi rice short-grain sushi rice
❖ 1 cup water
❖ 1 ½ tbsp. sushi vinegar (or 1 tbsp. rice vinegar, 1/2 tbsp. sugar, 1/2 tsp. salt)

For Unagi Sushi

❖ 4 oz unagi
❖ 1/2 cucumber cut into ½-inch strips
❖ 2 sheets nori seaweed
❖ 2 green onions
❖ sesame seeds

METHOD

Make Sushi Rice:

1. Rinse and wash the rice when it's time to cook. Then, water is added.
2. Put everything in a large dish and refrigerate it. While the mixture is still hot, add the sushi vinegar (or the mixture of rice vinegar, sugar and salt).

Cook Unagi:

1. Bake unagi for 10-12 minutes at 360 degrees Fahrenheit, or as indicated on the package. After that, use kitchen shears to cut it into 12-inch strips.

Make Unagi Sushi Roll:

1. Wrap the bamboo mat in plastic wrap and place it on a level surface (Disposal of rice clinging to the bamboo will be made easy thanks to this technique.).
2. Cut the nori sheets in thirds once they have been cut in half along the long axis.
3. It's important to make sure the bamboo's glossy side is facing down before placing half of a nori sheet on top of it.
4. Using around 3/4 cup rice, cover the nori with the rice. You may also add sesame seeds if you like. Immerse your hands in Tezu water* to prevent them from sticking.
5. Layer the unagi, cucumber, green onions, and any other preferred ingredients on the nori sheet after that (such as avocado).
6. To accomplish this, place your thumbs behind the bamboo pad and raise it up and over your teeth. As you roll the mat away from you, use your hands to push the rice and filling into the surface of the mat. Roll the

bamboo mat away from you as you press the rice and filling into the surface of the mat with your hands. If you want to finish rolling, do so until the ends meet.

7. With this method, you should be able to get eight pieces each roll.

8. Drizzle the roll with unagi sauce for an extra dose of flavor. Eat it right now to get the most enjoyment out of it.

20.PHILADELPHIA ROLL

Prep Time: 10 minutes | **Cook Time:** 1 hour | **Servings:** 4 Rolls

EQUIPMENT

- ❖ Bamboo Sushi Mat
- ❖ Plastic wrap, (optional)

INGREDIENTS

For Sushi Rice

- ❖ 1 cup sushi rice
- ❖ 1 cup water
- ❖ 1 ½ tablespoons optional sushi vinegar (1/2 tablespoon sugar, and 1/2 teaspoon salt)
- ❖ For Philadelphia Roll
- ❖ 4 oz smoked salmon
- ❖ 4 oz cream cheese (cut into ½-inch strips)
- ❖ 1/2 cucumber (cut into ½-inch strips)
- ❖ 2 sheets nori (seaweed sheet)
- ❖ 1 tablespoon sesame seeds (you can toast it in a hot skillet for a few minutes for extra flavor)

METHOD

1. To begin the process of cooking rice, rinse it and put it in a rice cooker with water. Put everything in a large dish and refrigerate it. Mixture is still hot, add sushi vinegar while it is still hot (or the mixture of rice vinegar, sugar and salt).
2. Take your sushi in Philadelphia to the next level by following these simple steps: Cover the bamboo mat with plastic wrap and set it on a level surface (this will prevent rice from sticking to the bamboo).
3. Add half of the nori sheet on top of the mat.
4. Make sure your hands are clean by dipping them in vinegar water before handling the cooked rice* (this will prevent rice from sticking to your palms). The distribution of nori is perfect.
5. Rice should now be facing down instead of up.
6. Cut the smoked salmon strips into half-inch pieces before serving.
7. Before adding the salmon and cream cheese, spread the nori with cream cheese and cucumber slices.
8. To accomplish this, place your thumbs behind the bamboo pad and raise it up and over your teeth.
9. Rolling the mat away from you and applying pressure to the edges can help you tighten the bamboo mat. If you want to finish rolling, do so until the ends meet.
10. The sesame seeds should be applied once the bamboo mat has been removed.
11. With this method, you should be able to get eight pieces each roll. Enjoy your meal when it's been served!

21.CATERPILLAR ROLL {WITH AN AVOCADO TOPPING}

Prep Time: 20 minute | **Cook Time:** 50 minute | **Servings:** 4 rolls

INGREDIENTS

For Sushi Rice

- ❖ 1 cup sushi rice short-grain sushi rice
- ❖ 1 cup water
- ❖ 1 tablespoon sushi vinegar (optional) or a mixture 1/2 tablespoon sugar and 1 tablespoon rice vinegar

For Caterpillar Rolls

- ❖ 4 oz unagi or, shrimp or tuna
- ❖ 1/2 cucumber cut into 1/2-inch strips
- ❖ 2 sheets nori (seaweed sheet)
- ❖ 2 avocado ripe but still firm

METHOD

1. Squeeze off any extra water from the rice after straining it to remove any debris. At this time, a Rice Maker should be filled with rice and water. Immediately after removing it from the fire, place it in a large bowl to cool down slightly. While the sauce is still quite hot, add the optional sushi vinegar (or the mixture of rice vinegar and sugar).
2. To get the best results, bake the unagi for 10-12 minutes at 360°F, or according to the package directions. Take a half-inch piece and cut it in half.
3. A bamboo mat or plastic wrap can be laid out on the table before the caterpillar rolls are prepared (this will make clean up easier).

4. Using a pair of scissors or your hands, cut the nori sheets in half.
5. Finally, half of the nori sheet should be laid on top of the bamboo.
6. Cover the nori with a third of a cup of cooked rice. (To prevent your hands from sticking, try dipping them in vinegar water.)
7. The rice should now be placed face down.
8. Unagi and cucumber strips should be placed on top of the nori.
9. To accomplish this, place your thumbs behind the bamboo pad and raise it up and over your teeth.
10. Rolling the mat away from you and applying pressure to the edges can help you tighten the bamboo mat. If you want to finish rolling, do so until the ends meet.
11. Slice an avocado in half to remove the pit and skin. After that, cut each half-moon in half.
12. NOW IS THE TIME TO GET WORK DONE!
13. Pull it up with a large knife and place it on top of the sushi.
14. On top of the plastic wrap, place the sushi mat. Make a roll out of the avocado by squeezing it out.
15. After removing the mat but preserving the plastic wrap, cut the roll into bite-sized pieces. Remove the plastic wrap to get started.

22. TAMAGO SUSHI RECIPE

Prep Time: 15 minute | **Cook Time:** 45 minute | **Servings:** 12 pieces

EQUIPMENT

- ❖ Tamagoyaki Omelette Pan
- ❖ Mixing Bowl

INGREDIENTS

For the Sushi Rice

- ❖ 1 cup sushi rice
- ❖ 1 cup water
- ❖ 1 ½ tablespoons optional sushi vinegar (1/2 tablespoon sugar)

For Tamagoyaki

- ❖ 4 eggs
- ❖ 2 tablespoon water
- ❖ 1/4 teaspoon rice vinegar
- ❖ 1 ½ tablespoon sugar
- ❖ 1 tablespoon mirin
- ❖ 1/4 teaspoon salt
- ❖ oil
- ❖ Other
- ❖ nori
- ❖ optional soy sauce for serving

METHOD

Cook Sushi Rice

1. Before adding the shrimp to the boiling water, season it with a pinch of salt. Put everything in a large dish and refrigerate it. Mixture is still hot, add sushi vinegar while it is still hot (or the mixture of rice vinegar, sugar, and salt).

Make Tamagoyaki for Sushi

1. Eggs are beaten in a bowl. Be careful not to overbeat the eggs.
2. A separate dish should be used to mix the water, rice vinegar, sugar, and mirin.
3. In a separate dish, combine the egg and spice ingredients and whisk them together. Mix the items together with a whisk. Use a sieve to remove grit from the egg mixture. Pour the ingredients into the pan as it cooks using a measuring cup with a spout and handle.
4. Pre-heating a rectangle tamagoyaki pan (or a round pan, see notes*) to medium-high heat is required before cooking the eggs. After that, use a folded paper towel to coat the pan in oil.
5. The oil should be heated to a temperature where an egg mixture with seasonings may be added. Allow the liquid to flow to the pan's rim by tilting the pan toward the liquid.
6. When the egg has cooled slightly but is still malleable, roll it into a log shape. If the egg is overdone, it will not attach to the log while rolling it up. Whether or whether your eggs are folded precisely doesn't matter.

7. After removing and wiping down the pan with a paper towel coated in extra oil, remove the rolled omelette. When you're ready to cook your omelette, brush it with some olive oil.
8. Add another layer of egg mixture to the bottom of the pan. Lifting the omelette will allow the mixture to flow beneath it.
9. It's time to roll the log back onto the egg once it's cooled down a bit and the top is still soft.
10. Stop cooking once you've used up all of the egg mixture.
11. Set the tamagoyaki on a sushi mat once you remove it from the pan. Before serving, shape the hot and ready-to-eat tamagoyaki into the desired shapes. Let it settle for about five minutes before using.
12. Once the tamagoyaki has been cut into 12 equal pieces, place it in a separate dish.

Make Tamago Sushi

1. Pieces of nori seaweed that are 14 inches wide Let it go for now.
2. Cook the rice and form it into a long oval shape, about 1 inch wide by 1 inch long. Squeeze the rice gently to flatten the bottom. If your hands get stuck, you might try dipping them in vinegar water to loosen them up.
3. To ensure that the tamagoyaki sticks to the rice, lay it on top and push down firmly.
4. Wrap the nori strip around the sushi's width to keep the tamagoyaki in place. 12 pieces can be made in this manner.
5. Lay out the Tamago sushi on a serving tray when you've finished putting it together. Adding soy sauce to the meal is optional.

23. HOMEMADE SUSHI PIZZA RECIPE

Prep Time: 15 minutes | **Cook Time:** 45 minutes | **Servings:** 4 slices

EQUIPMENT

- ❖ Bamboo Sushi Mat
- ❖ Plastic Wrap
- ❖ Cutting Board
- ❖ Kitchen Scissors

INGREDIENTS

For the Sushi Rice

- ❖ 2 cups sushi rice (uncooked short-grain sushi rice)
- ❖ 2 cups water
- ❖ 3 tablespoons sushi vinegar (or mixing 2 tablespoons of rice vinegar and 1 tablespoon of sugar)

For the Rolls & Crust

- ❖ 4 imitation crab stick
- ❖ 1-2 avocado
- ❖ 8 sheets nori (seaweed sheet)

For the Toppings

- ❖ 2 tablespoons sesame seeds
- ❖ 1 avocado sliced
- ❖ 8 oz salmon (sashimi-grade salmon, tuna, or shrimp)
- ❖ 1-2 cucumber
- ❖ optional mayonnaise

METHOD

Cook Sushi Rice

1. Rinse the sushi rice and add some water to the rice cooker. Put everything in a large dish and refrigerate it. While the mixture is still hot, slowly whisk in the sushi vinegar.

Make Sushi Rolls

1. Using plastic wrap, secure the bamboo mat to the table (this will make clean-up easier).
2. Dip your hands in a little cup of Tezu Vinegar Water* if they get stuck (normal water combined with a small amount of vinegar).
3. Cut the nori seaweed sheet in thirds with kitchen scissors. Tuck the final nori sheet into the mat's bottom, shiny side down.
4. A nori sheet at least half an inch thick and 3/4 cup of cooked rice are required for this recipe. Dip your fingers into the vinegar water and spread the rice out evenly.
5. Dividing the imitation crab stick in half horizontally is the easiest way to do this. The crab stick and avocado slices should be placed on top of the rice. It's amazing how much filling you can get away with using just a little.
6. To accomplish this, place your thumbs behind the bamboo pad and raise it up and over your teeth.
7. While pushing the rice and filling into the bamboo mat, roll it away from you. Stop rolling as soon as you reach the end of the bamboo mat.
8. As you roll the nori into a cylinder, you'll need to peel back the mat. When slicing the roll, carefully press the

mat to keep it from separating. Repeat the previous process for a total of four more rolls. Put an end to them.

Assemble Sushi Pizza

1. Slice a nori seaweed triangular piece into the shape of a pizza using a knife.
2. It's created by distributing a quarter of the rice onto a seaweed sheet and spreading it out evenly. Put a light pressure on the rice by gently pressing down on it.
3. Sesame seeds can be sprinkled on top if desired.
4. Place a sushi roll at the tip of the triangle-shaped pizza dough. Cut the ends of the roll-off to line the crust.
5. The sushi pizza comes complete with toppings of avocado, smoked salmon, and cucumber on top. Enjoy your meal when it's been served!

24. TUNA SUSHI ROLL

Prep time: 10 minute | **Cook time:** 15 minute | **Serves:** 8

INGREDIENTS

- ❖ 325 g tuna in oil
- ❖ 3 cups sushi rice
- ❖ 1/2 cup Kewpie mayonnaise
- ❖ 1/2 cup rice vinegar
- ❖ 2 tbsp sugar
- ❖ 2 tsp salt
- ❖ Handful green salad leaves
- ❖ 3 yaki nori seaweed sheets

Tools:

- ❖ Bamboo mat
- ❖ Cooking Directions

METHOD

1. To begin, we'll need to cook the rice. Add the sushi rice to a small saucepan half-filled with water. The rice and water should be cooked until they form a funnel shape on the stovetop at a high temperature. Wait for the sauce to thicken before lowering the heat and covering the pan. It will take another 10 to 15 minutes for the food to be done.

2. We'll prepare our tuna while the rice cooks. Draining the oil out of the tuna is as simple as opening the can. Pour 1/2 cup kewpie mayonnaise over the chunks of tuna and mix well with your hands. Use the amount of mayonnaise that you desire to achieve the greatest outcomes.

3. This recipe calls for 2 tbsp sugar, 2 tablespoons of rice vinegar in addition to the salt to season the rice.
4. A piece of rough seaweed should be placed on top of your bamboo mat.
5. Keep approximately an inch of seaweed visible at the top of the rice to provide visual interest. Wiping your hands with a moist cloth will help to keep them from becoming sticky.
6. To achieve this, arrange the filling in a column along the center of the rice.
7. As you begin to roll the sushi, the seaweed and bamboo sheets should guide each other. When rolling it up, use a little push to keep it in place. That concludes our discussion.

25.SPIDER ROLL RECIPE

Prep Time: 15 minute | **Cook Time:** 45 minute | **Servings:** 3 rolls

EQUIPMENT

- ❖ Bamboo Sushi Mat
- ❖ Plastic Wrap
- ❖ Dutch Oven
- ❖ Slotted Spoon

INGREDIENTS

For the Sushi Rice

- ❖ 1 cup sushi rice
- ❖ 1 cup water
- ❖ 1 ½ tablespoons optional sushi vinegar (1/2 tablespoon sugar)
- ❖ For the Crab Tempura
- ❖ 3 soft-shell crabs
- ❖ 1 large egg
- ❖ 3/4 cup iced water
- ❖ 1 cup all-purpose flour
- ❖ oil for frying

For the Spider Roll

- ❖ 1/2 cucumber (cut into thin strips, you can also use avocados)
- ❖ 1 carrots (cut into thin strips)
- ❖ 2 sheets nori (seaweed sheet)
- ❖ unagi sauce (to taste, optional)

METHOD

Cook Sushi Rice

1. Add the rice to the rice cooker with the water and let it simmer for a few minutes until it's done. Toss the food into a large bowl once it has cooled down. Mix in some sushi vinegar with a fork while the mixture is still heated.

Cook Crab Tempura

1. Place the oil to a large pot or Dutch oven and heat over medium-high heat.
2. Add the egg to a half-filled measuring cup of cold water.
3. Quickly combine the items in a mixing bowl by vigorously stirring them.
4. It's best to use a large bowl of flour for this task. Pour the ingredients into the blender in a steady stream. Use caution while combining ingredients. Don't over-mix your ingredients.
5. Once the crab has been well cleaned and dried, it is time to dip it in the batter and serve.
6. Fry the crab until golden brown, about a minute or two.
7. Place the cooked crab on a paper towel-lined dish and use a slotted spoon to remove any excess oil.

Make Spider Rolls

1. Wrap the bamboo mat with plastic wrap.
2. Using scissors, cut the nori sheet into two equal halves.
3. Add half of the nori sheet on top of the bamboo mat and push down firmly using the shiny side of the nori.
4. Spread roughly 3/4 cup of cooked rice on the nori sheet with your hands. Dip your hands in tezu water* to keep them wet.

5. The rice should now be placed face down.
6. One crab tempura roll should be placed on top of the nori, followed by three cucumber trips and three carrot trips. Serve with unagi sauce on the side, if desired.
7. To accomplish this, place your thumbs behind the bamboo pad and raise it up and over your teeth.
8. Rolling the mat away from you and applying pressure to the edges can help you tighten the bamboo mat. If you want to finish rolling, do so until the ends meet.
9. The plastic wrap and mat can be removed now. After then, the roll is divided into bite-sized pieces. The dish can be topped with a drizzle of soy sauce or unagi sauce. What are you doing now?

26.HOW TO MAKE OSHINKO ROLL

Prep Time: 1 hour | **Total Time:** 1 hour | **Servings:** 4 Rolls

EQUIPMENT

❖ Sushi Rolling Mat

INGREDIENTS

For sushi rice:

❖ 1 cup sushi rice Japanese short-grain rice such as California Calrose
❖ 1 cup water
❖ 1 ½ TBS SUSHI VINEGAR OR MIXING VINEGAR 1 teaspoon salt, 2 tablespoons rice vinegar, 1 tablespoon sugar

Oshinko sushi rolls:

- ❖ 10 oz yellow pickled radish (Takuan)
- ❖ 4 sheets nori seaweed sheet

Optional for Serving:

- ❖ soy sauce
- ❖ Wasabi paste

METHOD

Make the sushi rice

1. Remove any leftover scum by thoroughly rinsing the rice in cold water. The rice maker should be used to prepare the rice in accordance with the directions provided by the manufacturer.
2. Immediately after removing it from the fire, place it in a large bowl to cool down slightly. Mixture is still hot, add sushi vinegar while it is still hot (the mixture of rice vinegar, sugar, and salt). Let it go for now.

Make Oshinko sushi rolls

1. Slice the radish into 1/4-inch-thick slices lengthwise.
2. Put the bamboo mat on a level surface and wrap it with plastic wrap (this will make clean up easier).
3. The seaweed sheet should be cut in half. Lay the remaining nori sheet on top of the bamboo with the glossy side down.
4. Distribute 3/4 cup of cooked rice evenly over the nori sheet, leaving about 12 inches at the top for garnish. It is recommended that you use Tezu vinegar water to prevent stickiness.

5. Pickled radish slices should be served on the side of the rice. This is how many strips I use per wrap because my radish is so short. As many strips as the seaweed sheet if it's the same length.
6. To accomplish this, place your thumbs behind the bamboo pad and raise it up and over your teeth.
7. Roll the bamboo mat away from you to firmly combine the rice and its contents.
8. Top with wasabi and soy sauce if preferred.

27.SALMON SKIN ROLLS RECIPE

Servings: 4

INGREDIENTS

❖ Avocado
❖ Red Pepper
❖ Salmon fillets
❖ 1 teaspoon Sesame oil
❖ 4 tablespoon sweet chili sauce
❖ Nori sheets
❖ Cooked Sushi rice
❖ Mayonnaise
❖ Fish eggs

METHOD

1. Slicing the avocado in half will allow you to get at the seed. After removing the skin from the second half, cut it into slices 1 to 2 mm thick.
2. Keep the blade of your knife wet to make slicing simpler. Slice it with care to prevent damage to the avocado slices.

3. Cut the red pepper into long, thin slices, about 0.5 to 1 cm broad.
4. Using a sharp knife, remove the salmon skin off the fillets. Skin and 0.5 centimeters of salmon flesh should be removed.
5. Use a nonstick pan to fry the salmon skin without the use of any oil at all. Put 1 teaspoon of sesame oil to the pieces after they've been browned and crispy. After giving it a good stir, let it cook for a few seconds to release the steam. After that, stir in 4 tablespoons of sweet chili sauce. Before stirring, let the chile to become aromatic. To avoid overcooking the sauce, remove it from the heat and set it aside.
6. Place a little bit of rice in the center of the nori sheet after dipping your hands in water. To accommodate the rice, leave a third of the page blank.
7. Wrap the nori with cling wrap before serving. The rice nori should be flipped over so that the rice-covered side is facing you using cling film.
8. Arrange the crispy salmon skin and red pepper strips on top of the sheet's white section. Flip over the nori and cling film with the ingredients and place them on the empty section.
9. When rolling the sushi, gently push it toward the filling using the bamboo mat. The cling film should be removed from the mat once you've rolled the dough. Continue the same with the remaining rolls.
10. Once the cling film has been removed, the avocado slices can be placed on your hand. Take care to put it right on top of the mayonnaise. Re-seal the cling film after placing a pad on top of the avocado. When rolling the avocado, use pressure to keep it in place.

11. Cut the roll into seven or eight sections and two end pieces using cling film. Add a few fish eggs and a large quantity of sweet chili sauce to each piece before serving. What are you doing now?

28.CUCUMBER ROLL

Total time: 45 minutes | **Servings**: 5 rolls

INGREDIENTS

FOR THE QUICK PICKLED CARROTS

- ❖ ½ cup apple cider vinegar
- ❖ ½ cup water
- ❖ 2 tablespoons sugar
- ❖ 1 tablespoon kosher salt
- ❖ 2 large carrots, cut into matchsticks

FOR THE SPICY MAYO

- ❖ ½ cup vegan mayonnaise
- ❖ 2 teaspoons sriracha, or to taste
- ❖ 1 teaspoon soy sauce, optional
- ❖ 1 teaspoon lime juice, optional

FOR THE SUSHI RICE

- ❖ 1 ½ cups sushi rice (see notes)
- ❖ 1 ½ cups water
- ❖ 2 tablespoons rice vinegar
- ❖ 1 tablespoon granulated sugar
- ❖ ½ teaspoon kosher salt

FILLING

- ❖ 5 sheets of Nori
- ❖ Quick Pickled Carrot (from above)
- ❖ 1 cucumber, cut into matchsticks
- ❖ 1 avocado, sliced
- ❖ Sesame seeds, for garnish

METHOD

FOR THE QUICK PICKLED CARROTS

1. A small, heatproof dish should be used to combine the apple cider vinegar, water, sugar, and salt. The microwave should be able to handle this in around 2 minutes.
2. Put the carrots in a jar or other airtight container. Refrigerate the carrots for at least ten minutes before serving after pouring the liquid mixture over them.

FOR THE SPICY MAYO

1. A small serving is all you need. Once you've prepared to use it, store it in an airtight container.

FOR THE SUSHI RICE

1. Your rice should be crystal transparent after two minutes of washing.
2. Use a rice cooker and follow the manufacturer's instructions for adding the rice and water, and then cooking the rice.
3. Rice and water should be put on the stove and heated to a boil before they can be served. With the cover on, cook at a low temperature. After that, wait 10 minutes before serving the rice.

4. Rice vinegar, sugar, and salt should be combined in a microwave-safe bowl. After roughly a minute in the microwave, the sugar and salt should be completely dissolved.
5. As soon as it's cool enough to handle, pour the mixture over the rice and stir continuously for about 7 minutes. You only need a tiny amount. Storage in an airtight container until it's ready to use.

TO MAKE THE ROLLS

1. Wrap a sushi rolling mat with plastic to prevent it from being damaged (this will help keep it clean).
2. A nori sheet should be placed over the rolling mat before rolling begins. Cover the sushi mat entirely on three sides with a third of a cup of sushi rice, leaving about an inch of nori exposed on the side facing away from you.
3. A few slivers of carrot, cucumber, and avocado can be added to the nori closest to you!
4. You'll need a roll of Nori to cover the filling, and then roll it up as tightly as possible to the end of the rice.
5. Roll to seal the nori after applying water to the last inch of it. Sealing the roll may be done with the sushi mat.
6. Depending on how big you want your slices to be, cut six to eight out of the rolls of bread. As a finishing touch, sesame seeds and hot mayo go well with this meal.
7. It's time to savor.

29.SWEET POTATO ROLL SUSHI RECIPE

Prep Time: 15 minute | **Cook Time:** 1 hours | **Servings:** 3 rolls

EQUIPMENT

- ❖ Bamboo Sushi Mat
- ❖ Plastic Wrap
- ❖ Baking Sheet
- ❖ Sushi Rice

INGREDIENTS

For sushi rice:

- ❖ 1 cup sushi rice
- ❖ 1 cup water (This proportion yields rice that is neither excessively firm nor mushy)
- ❖ 1 ½ tablespoons sushi vinegar (or mixing 2 tablespoons rice vinegar, 1 tablespoon sugar, and 1 teaspoon salt)

Sweet potato sushi rolls:

- ❖ 1 large sweet potato
- ❖ 1 tablespoon vegetable oil
- ❖ 3 sheets nori (seaweed)
- ❖ 1 avocado ripe but still firm
- ❖ You may toast white sesame seeds in a pan over low heat for a few minutes until they're gently toasted.

Optional for Serving:

- ❖ soy sauce
- ❖ wasabi paste

METHOD

Make the sushi rice

1. Remove any leftover scum by thoroughly rinsing the rice in cold water. Add it to the rice cooker with water. To the letter, follow the recipe's directions. A rice cooker isn't required to cook rice on the stovetop.
2. Immediately after removing it from the fire, place it in a large bowl to cool down slightly. Mixture is still hot, add sushi vinegar while it is still hot (the mixture of rice vinegar, sugar, and salt).

Bake sweet potatoes

1. After peeling, slice the sweet potato into 1/2-inch-thick pieces.
2. They should be soft and delicate after 25 minutes of baking, during which time you should flip them over.
3. Allow for thorough cooling before using in sushi rolls.

Make sweet potato sushi rolls

1. The bamboo mat should be placed flat and covered with plastic wrap if desired (this will make clean-up easier). Make sure you have a bowl of Tezu vinegar water** (regular water mixed with a little bit of vinegar) on hand to protect your hands from becoming stuck.
2. Cut the nori seaweed sheet in thirds with kitchen scissors. Putting down the final nori sheet at the bottom of the mat is now complete.
3. A nori sheet at least half an inch thick and 3/4 cup of cooked rice are required for this recipe. Dip your fingers into the vinegar water and spread the rice out evenly. Applying too much pressure can result in soggy rice.

4. Before serving, sprinkle sesame seeds and avocado slices over the rice (towards the bottom, see the photo below). Proceed with caution if your roll won't shut properly due to an excessive amount of filling.
5. To accomplish this, place your thumbs behind the bamboo pad and raise it up and over your teeth.
6. While pushing the rice and filling into the bamboo mat, roll it away from you. Stop rolling when you reach the end of the bamboo mat.
7. As you roll the nori into a cylinder, you'll need to peel back the mat. When slicing the roll, carefully press the mat to keep it from separating.
8. After laying the roll on a cutting board, cut the roll's edges using a long, sharp knife. Make six or eight slices out of each bun. As a condiment, soy sauce and wasabi might be presented.

30.FUTOMAKI – THICK SUSHI ROLLS

Prep Time: 30 Minute | **Cook Time:** 15 Minute | **Servings:** 5 Rolls

INGREDIENTS

- ❖ 5 sheets nori
- ❖ 1 English seedless cucumber (cut into long thin 6½ inch (16.5cm) strips)
- ❖ 1 avocado (peeled, pitted, and sliced into strips)
- ❖ 1 packet Nova lox (sliced into strips) (3 oz/85g)
- ❖ Soy sauce for serving
- ❖ Wasabi for serving (optional)
- ❖ Pickled ginger optional

Sushi Rice

- ❖ 2 cups medium-grain rice (400g)
- ❖ 2½ cups water (600ml)
- ❖ 1 piece kombu (wiped with damp paper towel) (about 2-in x 2-in square)

Vinegar Mixture

- ❖ 6 tbsp rice vinegar
- ❖ 4 tbsp sugar
- ❖ 1 tsp salt

METHOD

Sushi Rice

1. Rinse and drain rice four or five times in a medium pot. Rice should be soaked in water for 20 minutes. Drain.
2. Pour in 212 glasses of water (600 ml). Delete the saucepan from the heat and add the kombu when it has

come to a boil. When water begins to boil, remove kombu from it. Before putting the lid back on, be sure the water is boiling. On a medium-low heat, cook the rice for about 10 minutes, or until all of the water has evaporated.

3. To turn off the burner, turn it off without lifting the cover from the pot. Let the rice sit for at least 10 minutes before you begin to work with it.
4. Vinegar, sugar, and salt should be combined in a small basin for this recipe. Stir sugar and salt in a bowl with boiling water until they're fully dissolved.
5. After the rice has been wet, transfer it to a sushi tub or a big shallow bowl. Toss the rice with a generous amount of vinegar. Use a rice paddle to incorporate the vinegar mixture into the batter. Mash attempts are not permitted.
6. Using a paddle and a fan, make sure the rice is constantly being rotated. As a result, the rice will soak up more vinegar and seem glossier.

Making the rolls and serving

1. Sushi Mat: Use this as a working surface. Place a sheet of nori on the mat with the shiny side facing up, matching the edge closest to you with the mat. Make sure to reserve 112 inches of nori for your completed product after moistening your hands and applying a thin coating of vinegared rice using the rice paddle. At this stage, the rice should be approximately one-fourth inch tall. If you construct a ridge at the end of the container, the filling will not roll forward.
2. Stack three slices of avocado and several strips of lox in the centre of the rice.
3. Keep your fingertips on the filling as you roll the mat ahead to prevent spillage. You should keep the nori seam

at the bottom of the mat while you continue rolling and then begin to re-retract the mat in the other direction.

4. Make a fist with your palms and squeeze the mat hard to compress the roll. Keep the filling in the middle and avoid shoving it all the way out at the ends. This technique should be repeated as many times as the rice may be used until it runs out.
5. Slice each sushi roll into six equal halves.
6. All you need to serve this meal is a little soy sauce, some wasabi, and some pickled ginger.

31.GODZILLA ROLL RECIPE

Prep Time: 15 mins | **Cook Time:** 45 minutes | **Servings:** 3 rolls

EQUIPMENT

❖ Bamboo Sushi Mat
❖ Plastic Wrap

INGREDIENTS

For Sushi Rice

❖ Short-grain sushi rice, 1 cup
❖ 1 cup water
❖ 1 ½ tbsp. sushi vinegar (or 1 tbsp. rice vinegar, 1/2 tbsp. sugar, 1/2 tsp. salt)

For Godzilla Roll

❖ 6 oz pre-cooked shrimp tempura (about 8 pieces)
❖ ½ cucumber cut into thin slices
❖ 1 avocado cut into thin slices

- ❖ 2 sheets nori seaweed

Optional for Serving:

- ❖ spicy mayo
- ❖ masago
- ❖ soy sauce

METHOD

Make Sushi Rice:

1. Rice should be rinsed before it is put into a rice cooker, along with the water. Follow the directions on the package exactly.
2. Put everything in a large dish and refrigerate it. While the mixture is still hot, add the sushi vinegar (or the mixture of rice vinegar, sugar and salt).

Make Godzilla Rolls:

1. To keep your bamboo mat clean, cover it with plastic wrap. It will be easy to keep your mat clean if you do this.
2. Cut the nori seaweed sheet in thirds with kitchen scissors.
3. Bottom-facing glossy side of leftover nori sheet should face the mat's surface.
4. A nori sheet at least half an inch thick and 3/4 cup of cooked rice are required for this recipe. Using Tezu water*, you can wash your hands before to distributing rice.
5. The grains need to be evenly distributed. Rice becomes mushy if pressure is applied excessively.
6. The rice can be topped with sliced avocados and cucumbers.

7. To accomplish this, place your thumbs behind the bamboo pad and raise it up and over your teeth. While pushing the rice and filling into the bamboo mat, roll it away from you. If you want to finish rolling, do so until the ends meet.
8. Divide the sushi roll in half horizontally and vertically to produce 8 servings. Eat it right now to get the most enjoyment out of it.

32. TEKKA NORI MAKI (TUNA ROLL)

Servings: 4

INGREDIENTS

Sushi rice

- ❖ 3 cups cooked Japanese rice
- ❖ 40 ml rice vinegar
- ❖ 1 tablespoon sugar
- ❖ 3/4 teaspoon salt

For rolls

- ❖ 6-8 oz Tuna sashimi

METHOD

1. Cooked rice should be mixed with rice vinegar, sugar, and salt in a container. Make sure everything is well combined.
2. Make sure to add rice vinegar to your bamboo mat's soaking water.

3. Stack up a nori sheet and place it on a bamboo mat with the shiny side facing down. Put 1 cup of rice in the center of the nori sheet, moistening your hands with vinegar water.
4. With your fingertips, evenly distribute the rice on the nori sheet.
5. tuna fillets cut into tiny slices (as long as possible)
6. Nori and tuna should be laid out on a level surface.
7. With your thumbs, grip the mat's bottom edges and use your other fingers to hold the toppings in place.
8. As you roll the bamboo mat into a cylindrical form, lift the mat's edges to hold the filling in place. You should see a letter C as you roll along the mat. Allow yourself some wiggle room when you're ready to stop rolling.
9. To make eating on the fly a little simpler, cut the roll in half and then in thirds.
10. Wasabi and soy sauce might be added to the dish for additional flavor.

33.HOMEMADE UNAGI SUSHI ROLLS ORIGINAL RECIPE

Servings: 4

INGREDIENTS

FOR THE RICE

- ❖ 1 Cup of cup sushi rice sushi rice (short-grain)
- ❖ 2 TBSP of tablespoons sushi vinegar
- ❖ 1 Cup of water

FOR UNAGI

- ❖ 4 oz of Unagi
- ❖ 2 nori seaweed sheets
- ❖ ½ of cucumber (cut into ½-inch strips)
- ❖ sesame seeds (to your liking)
- ❖ 2 onions
- ❖ Unagi sauce (see recipe here)

INSTRUCTIONS

FOR THE SUSHI RICE:

1. Rinse the rice completely before placing it in the rice cooker. Incorporate some water into the mixture.
2. After the rice has finished cooking, it should be moved to a large bowl. Cool down a little bit. It's easiest to blend sushi vinegar, rice vinegar, sugar, and salt while they're still warm.

FOR UNAGI

1. Using a 360F oven, bake the unagi for around 10 minutes. Make half-inch-wide strips out of the material.

UNAGI SUSHI ROLL

1. Plastic wrap the bamboo mat to prevent rice from sticking.
2. Cut the nori sheets in half using a pair of scissors.
3. Using the shiny side down, place half of a nori sheet on the bamboo. Then, push down hard to adhere.
4. About 3/4 cup of rice should be put evenly on top of nori. Sesame seeds can also be added. In order to protect your hands from sticking, immerse them in Tezu water*.
5. Cucumber and onion slices, or even avocado, can be placed in the center of the baking pan.
6. The thumbs should not be placed on top of the bamboo mat. To use the filling, lift the edge and roll it over the filling. Remove the bamboo mat from your body by rolling it away. Press the rice and stuffing together until well combined. Keep the ball going to the end.
7. The number of pieces per roll should be eight.
8. To amp up the taste of your sushi roll, drizzle a little unagi sauce over the top. Savor the moment.

34.HAWAIIAN SUSHI ROLLS RECIPE

Prep time: 1 hour | **Cook time:** 20 minute | **Servings:** 4

INGREDIENTS

- ❖ 2 sheets of nori
- ❖ 2 cups cooked sushi rice
- ❖ 1 tablespoon toasted sesame seeds
- ❖ 2 (6-ounce) lobster tails, removed from shells, cut into 1/2-inch-thick pieces
- ❖ 1 ripe mango, pitted, peeled, sliced into thin strips
- ❖ 1/2 of 1 English cucumber, quartered, cored, and julienned
- ❖ 1 ripe avocado, peeled, pitted, and sliced into thin strips
- ❖ Wasabi
- ❖ Soy sauce

METHOD

1. To preserve a bamboo sushi mat from the outdoors, wrap it with plastic wrap. Lay down the nori sheet to make a sushi mat. A thin coating of sushi rice should be spread over the nori. Make sure the rice is covered in sesame seeds. It's time to flip the nori over and face you. It is best to arrange the lobster in the center of the nori. Add chopped mango and avocado to the mix. Roll up firmly using the bamboo mat as a guide, giving a few soft squeezes along the way. Make 8 sushi rolls with the ingredients you've already prepared. Add the other ingredients and mix well. Repeat the steps.

35.GOLDEN AVOCADO SUSHI ROLL

Cook time: 30 minute | **Total time:** 30 minute | **Servings:** 2 rolls

INGREDIENTS

- ❖ 2 nori wraps
- ❖ 1 cup cooked brown rice, short-grain
- ❖ 1/2 tsp turmeric
- ❖ 1/4 tsp tamari
- ❖ 2 tsp maple syrup, grade B
- ❖ 1/2 avocado thinly sliced
- ❖ 8-10 strips bell pepper, thinly chopped
- ❖ 2 tsp fresh orange juice (sub seasoned rice vinegar)
- ❖ pinch ginger, grated
- ❖ pinch flat-leaf parsley, finely chopped
- ❖ pinch cayenne (optional)
- ❖ 2 tsp pumpkin seeds (optional)

METHOD

1. Combine the rice, turmeric, maple syrup, and tamari in a small bowl. Serve with a sauce that is orange in hue.
2. Approximately two-thirds of the nori wrap's surface should be covered by rice. Slices of avocado and bell pepper can be added. After spreading a teaspoon of orange juice over top, you may add the optional ginger, parsley, and cayenne pepper to taste.
3. If you want to make a nori burrito, just coil the nori sheet into a burrito shape, but leave the ends exposed. Slice it after at least two minutes of resting. Rice should face up when slicing the rolls into 1-inch circles. If you choose, you may serve the meal with

wasabi and ginger on top. Just a few slices of orange might be OK, if you'd like. Whether you sprinkle pumpkin seeds on top of the rolls, on them, or even inside them is all up to you.

36.VEGAN RAINBOW SUSHI ROLLS

Time: 50 Mins | **Servings:** 20 Rolls

INGREDIENTS

- ❖ 300g sushi rice
- ❖ 100ml rice wine vinegar
- ❖ 2 tbsp golden caster sugar
- ❖ 1 pack of Nori seaweed
- ❖ 1 cucumber
- ❖ 1 red pepper
- ❖ 1 avocado
- ❖ 1 mango
- ❖ 30g sushi ginger
- ❖ 15g wasabi
- ❖ 1 jar of Baxters Spicy Jalapeno Chilli Relish

METHOD

1. The product instructions for sushi rice should be followed.
2. Using the same ways, reduce the amount of rice wine vinegar and sugar by half.
3. Vinegar should be reduced before serving, and should only be added at the last minute.
4. After the cucumber has been peeled and deseeded, cut it into long strips.

5. There should be long strips of peeled and sliced mangoes on the plate.
6. Make long strips of pepper by slicing it into long pieces.
7. When you want to make long strips out of an avocado, you'll need to cut it in half and remove the stone.
8. With damp hands, place a nori sheet on a bamboo sushi mat and wrap it up.
9. Using your palms, spread a thin coating of rice on the nori sheet and smooth it down into a thin layer
10. The vegetables, ginger, and wasabi should be arranged in a single row in the middle of the rice.
11. When you're done, carefully lift the mat's end and roll it softly over the contents.
12. Roll it all the way forward to complete the roll.
13. Add the other ingredients and mix well.
14. Start by slicing some hot Jalapeno Chilli Relish!

37.CREAM CHEESE AND CRAB SUSHI ROLLS

Total Time: 1 hr 40 mins | **Servings:** 2

INGREDIENT

- ❖ 1 cup uncooked white rice
- ❖ 2 cups water
- ❖ 2 tablespoons rice vinegar
- ❖ 1 teaspoon salt
- ❖ 2 sheets nori seaweed sheets
- ❖ ¼ cucumber, peeled and sliced lengthwise
- ❖ 2 pieces imitation crab legs
- ❖ ½ (3 ounce) package cream cheese, sliced
- ❖ 1 teaspoon minced fresh ginger root

INSTRUCTIONS

1. Bring the rice and water to a boil in a saucepan over high heat. For 20 to 25 minutes, lower the heat to medium-low, cover, and allow the rice to absorb the liquid. In a bowl, combine the rice vinegar and salt. Before usage, allow the product to cool fully.

2. Stack a few sheets of seaweed on the dining table. Spread the rice equally across each sheet, leaving a half-inch gap on one longitudinal side. Wet your hands and proceed. Line up cucumber slices, imitation crabmeat, and cream cheese in a straight line on the other side of the gap. The sushi should be rolled from the end of the seaweed sheet to the end of the toppings.

3. With a sharp, moist knife, cut each roll into five or six pieces. Serve with a garnish of sliced ginger on the side

38. EASY AVOCADO AND MANGO SUSHI ROLL

Prep Time: 20 mins | **Total Time:** 20 mins | **Servings:** 5 rolls

INGREDIENTS

- ❖ 1 large California Avocado thinly sliced
- ❖ 1 large Cucumber thinly sliced
- ❖ 1 head cauliflower riced
- ❖ 1 head Purple Cabbage thinly sliced
- ❖ 1 large Mango thinly sliced
- ❖ 1 large Carrots thinly sliced

INSTRUCTIONS

1. Stack 2/3 of the nori wrap with a thin layer of cauliflower rice on top of it.
2. On the nori sheet, put your cabbage, carrots, cucumbers, California avocado, and mango roughly 3/4 of the way down.
3. The nori wrap should be rolled up securely, beginning with the edge that is closest to your mouth or nose. Add just enough water to seal the nori roll's far edge. (You may use a sushi mat if you have one.)
4. Use a very sharp knife to cut the sushi into quarters. Serve with low sodium soy sauce or coconut aminos as a dipping sauce.

39.SOUTHWEST RICE ROLLS

Prep-Time: 50 Mins | **Total Time:** 2 Hours | **Servings:** 40 Pieces

INGREDIENTS

- ❖ 1½ cups short-grain brown rice
- ❖ ½ cup tomato sauce
- ❖ 2 teaspoons chili powder
- ❖ 1 teaspoon garlic powder
- ❖ 5 8-inch-square sheets nori (seaweed)
- ❖ 1 avocado, thinly sliced
- ❖ 1 cup bite-size strips red bell pepper
- ❖ 1 fresh jalapeño, seeded and cut into bite-size strips
- ❖ 1 cup chopped fresh tomatoes
- ❖ ¼ cup finely chopped red onion
- ❖ ¼ cup snipped fresh cilantro
- ❖ 2 tablespoons fresh lime juice (from about 1 lime)
- ❖ ¼ teaspoon sea salt
- ❖ Lime wedges

INSTRUCTIONS

1. Heat a 10-inch skillet over medium heat. After adding the rice, cook and stir for one minute. 3 quarts of water, tomato sauce, chili powder, and garlic powder, mixed together. In a large stock pot, bring water to a boil over high heat, stirring often. Reduce the temperature to medium-low. Cover the pan and cook for 45 minutes. Allow it cool for 10 minutes, covered, before serving. On a baking sheet, let the rice to cool to room temperature.

2. Sushi mats covered with plastic wrap are needed for each roll of nori. Use damp fingertips to evenly

sprinkle 1 scant cup rice to within 1 inch of the sheet's top border. Set aside a portion of the rice for the avocados, bell peppers, and jalapenos. The bottom border should be rolled up and pressed to seal the seam, if required. Cut each roll into eight equal pieces. Assemble and place in an attractive dish for serving.

3. Cucumber and lime juice should be combined with the tomatoes and onion in a small bowl. Serve the nori rolls alongside salsa and lime wedges.

40.NEW YORK ROLL

Prep time: 10 minutes | **Total time:** 15 minutes | **Servings:** 4

INGREDIENTS

- ❖ 3 cups cooked Japanese rice
- ❖ 40 ml Rice vinegar
- ❖ 1 tablespoon Sugar
- ❖ 3/4 teaspoon salt
- ❖ Ingredients for rolls
- ❖ 6 oz Cooked shrimp
- ❖ 1 Cucumber
- ❖ 1 Avocado
- ❖ 3 Nori (dried seaweed) sheets
- ❖ Sesame seeds

INSTRUCTIONS

1. In a bowl, mix together the cooked rice with the rice vinegar, sugar, and salt before thoroughly squeezing the mixture into the container.

2. To prevent rice from sticking to the bamboo mat, place a basin of water mixed with a little rice vinegar to the side.
3. This is what happened next: Place 1 cup of rice and a nori sheet on the bamboo mat, shiny side down.
4. The rice should be uniformly distributed on the nori sheet if your fingers are wet with vinegar water.
5. When the rice is done cooking, add about half a teaspoon of sesame seeds to it.
6. Slide the nori sheet near the bottom edge of the bamboo mat after flipping it over so the rice is facing down.
7. Make a line across the nori sheet with the cucumber, shrimp, and avocado once they've been chopped into stick-sized chunks.
8. Grab the mat's bottom edges with your thumbs, and the rest of your fingers with the toppings with your other fingers.
9. Begin by rolling the bamboo mat into a tight cylinder while raising the edges of the cylinder.
10. Continue rolling with a tiny touch of pressure and release when the roll is finished.
11. After cutting your New York Roll into three pieces on a cutting board, you're ready to cook.
12. Use soy sauce and wasabi, or any other dipping sauce of your choice, on your New York Roll to serve your guests.

41.SUSHI-STUFFED OCEAN TROUT WITH WASABI BUTTER

Prep time: 35 minutes | **Cook time:** 50 minutes | **Servings:** 6

INGREDIENTS

- ❖ 2 tbsp olive oil
- ❖ 1 onion, finely chopped
- ❖ 2 small red chillies, seeded, chopped
- ❖ 1 tbsp fresh grated ginger
- ❖ 3 cups cooked sushi rice
- ❖ 2 tbsp seasoned rice wine vinegar (see Notes)
- ❖ 2 tbsp chopped fresh coriander
- ❖ 2 tbsp fish sauce
- ❖ 1 1/2-2kg trout boned, butterflied (ask your fishmonger to do this)
- ❖ 6 sheets of nori (see Notes)
- ❖ 125g unsalted butter
- ❖ 2 tbsp lime juice
- ❖ 4 kaffir lime leaves, shredded
- ❖ 2 tbsp sliced pickled ginger
- ❖ Select all ingredients

METHOD

1. Bake at 180 degrees Celsius for about 30 minutes.
2. 1 tbsp. oil, heated in a small pan.
3. Unsure about the amount you'll require?
4. If you want to see the number, click on the underlined portion. Getting back and forth between the two locations is unnecessary!
5. Now that I've placed it on the cooktop, I'll turn the heat down. Before adding the onion, chili, and ginger, cook for

2-3 minutes to soften the onion. Coriander and fish sauce should be added to a bowl along with the cooked rice.

6. Load the fish cavity with the rice mixture after removing the fish's center cut. Bring the sides together to round the filling. Lay down nori sheets on the work surface and gradually overlap the edges to create a massive square. Fold the edges of the nori around the filleted fish. Use the remaining oil to assist the nori stick to your skin. On a lightly greased baking sheet, bake the fish for 30-40 minutes (depending on the fish's size). Check to see whether the skin gives easily by sticking a fork through it). Allow yourself some time to unwind.

7. Mix together the kaffir lime leaves and butter in a skillet over medium heat until the butter has melted and the sauce has started to crackle, then remove from the heat.

8. Serving suggestion: Garnish with pickled ginger and a drizzle of sauce on the side.

42.PHILADELPHIA ROLL

Servings: 4

INGREDIENTS

- ❖ 2 cups sushi rice (460 g)
- ❖ ¼ cup seasoned rice vinegar (60 mL)
- ❖ 4 half sheets sushi-grade nori
- ❖ 4 oz smoked salmon (115 g)
- ❖ 4 oz cream cheese (115 g), cut into matchsticks
- ❖ 1 small cucumber, cut into matchsticks

PREPARATION

1. To bring the sushi rice to room temperature, fan it and mix it with the rice vinegar.
2. Make sure the rough side of one nori sheet is facing up on the rolling mat before rolling.
3. Using damp hands, place a small amount of rice on top of the nori sheet. You don't want to smash the rice down, so spread it out evenly over the nori sheet.
4. Arrange the cream cheese and cucumber slices 1 inch (2 cm) from the bottom of the plate, followed by the smoked salmon and cream cheese.
5. Make a nice tight roll by squeezing down on the mat and the nori, ensuring that the surplus space at the bottom touches the opposite side. Make sure to squeeze the roll as you go so that it doesn't keep its original shape.
6. Cut the roll open with a knife on a cutting board. Rub a damp paper towel on the knife before slicing the roll in half.
7. Enjoy!

43.JAPANESE RAINBOW ROLL

Prep Time: 10 minute | **Total Time:** 10 minute | **Servings:** 1 roll

INGREDIENTS

- ❖ 3 pieces sashimi-grade salmon sliced thinly
- ❖ 3 pieces sashimi grade tuna sliced thinly
- ❖ 1 avocado sliced thinly same size as the fish, plus pieces for inside roll
- ❖ 2 pieces imitation crab meat
- ❖ 1 cucumber peeled and sliced lengthwise
- ❖ Prepared sushi rice see soft shell crab hand roll recipe on how to make sushi rice
- ❖ 1 piece of nori seaweed sheet
- ❖ Eel sauce Store-bought

INSTRUCTIONS

1. Place a piece of seaweed on your work surface with the smooth side up.
2. The sushi rice you produce should cover the seaweed to a depth of at least 80%. Spreads to the edges when rolled (as expected).
3. The counter should have a sushi-rolling mat on it.
4. Using a piece of plastic wrap, place a layer of rice on top of a piece of seaweed, then cover the meat with plastic.
5. The bottom third of the roll should be filled with cucumber, avocado, and imitation crab.
6. Roll it up using your sushi rolling mat.
7. As you place each piece of fish and avocado on top, switch it around.
8. Using the plastic wrap and rolling mat, gently re-roll the fish and avocado pieces on the roll.

9. Use a very sharp knife to cut the roll into 8 equal pieces.
10. Dip each piece of sushi in the sauce and serve. Dip it with soy and wasabi if you can't obtain the eel sauce you want.
11. Make the most of your time with it and attempt it!

44.SHAGGY DOG ROLL SUSHI

Prep Time: 10 mins | **Total Time:** 30 mins | **Servings:** 5 rolls

INGREDIENTS

❖ Shaggy Dog Roll Ingredients
❖ 3 cups white sushi rice
❖ 1/4 cup sushi rice seasoning
❖ 5-6 sheets Nori paper
❖ 1 package crab meat
❖ 5 tempura shrimp
❖ 2 avocados
❖ 7 sticks imitation crab

Optional toppings:

❖ 2-3 Tablespoon sesame seeds
❖ 1-2 teaspoon spicy mayo
❖ 1-2 teaspoon teriyaki sauce
❖ 1 teaspoon Sriracha
❖ 1-2 teaspoon chopped green onion

INSTRUCTIONS

1. Sushi rice can be made in the following ways:
2. Add enough water to cover the rice in a large mixing bowl. The rice should be soaked for a few minutes before cooking. Repeat this method until the water is clear.
3. Prepare the rice as directed on the container, or use a rice maker if you have one.
4. Stir in the sushi rice seasoning with a large wooden spoon after the rice has finished cooking. The rice needs 20 minutes to cool.
5. To create the roll:
6. While the rice cools, cut the crab into 1/4-inch pieces. Cut the avocado into strips after removing the peel.
7. Gather about the size of a palm's worth of rice and form it into a ball. (When working with sushi rice, I find it helpful to have a small bowl of water nearby.) Wet your fingertips before handling the rice to prevent it from sticking to your hands. The more you roll your sushi, the more you'll need to).
8. Cover the whole Nori sheet with a single ball of rice, being sure to cover all the corners. 1/2 cup water "Leave one side of the nori sheet uncovered as this will be how you seal your roll. Ensure that the nori side is on top, and the rice side is at the bottom.
9. Layer rice down the middle of your nori sheet. 4 tbsp crab meat, a tempura shrimp, and 2 avocado slices complete this dish (cut in half, with each half on the outside of avocado and crab meat)

10. Tuck in the nori's edges as you roll, starting at the rice-covered side and working your way outward. It's time to wet your fingers and spread water over the nori's 1/2-inch border before you're done rolling it. This moist edge

will adhere to the outside of the roll as it dries, making it waterproof.

11. Put a sushi mat on top and gently press it to tighten your roll. After removing the sushi mat, twist the roll 1/4 turn and then re-tighten the sushi mat. Do it as many times as you need to.

12. Putting it all together, we have the following:

13. In a microwave-safe container, heat the crab sticks in 2-piece batches for 10-15 seconds each.

14. Remove the crab sticks from the microwave and place them on a cutting board. Crab sticks should be halved and flattened on a cutting board before cooking. Place crab sticks that have been flattened on top of the roll before rolling it up.

15. Close the sushi mat around the sushi roll and crab with care.

16. Using a sushi knife or chef's knife, cut the roll into six to eight equal pieces.

17. Top with teriyaki sauce, sesame seeds, and hot mayo, if preferred. Add Sriracha and/or chopped green onions for a smoky flavor.

45.JAMBALAYA SUSHI ROLL

Prep Time: 15 Minutes | **Cook Time:** 5 Minutes | **Serves:** 2 People

INGREDIENTS

Jambalaya Roll

- ❖ 2 Links Andouille sausage
- ❖ 4 logs Imitation crab meat
- ❖ 1/2 Red Bell Pepper
- ❖ 1 stalk Celery
- ❖ 1/4 cup Garlic olive oil
- ❖ 1 teaspoon Garlic
- ❖ 1/2 cup Red onion
- ❖ 1 Roma tomato
- ❖ To taste Louisiana hot sauce
- ❖ 4 sheets Nori (Seaweed)
- ❖ 3 cups Sushi rice
- ❖ 3 teaspoon Creole Spice
- ❖ 2 tablespoon Black sesame seeds
- ❖ 2 tablespoon Pickled ginger
- ❖ 2 tablespoon Wasabi sauce
- ❖ Japanese Creole Sauce
- ❖ 1/2 cup Real mayo
- ❖ 3 tablespoon Louisiana hot sauce
- ❖ 1 teaspoon Key lime juice
- ❖ 1 teaspoon Garlic juice

PREPARATION

Jambalaya Roll

1. Make the sushi rice according to the package directions. Cooking rice in a rice cooker yields the greatest results.

Preparation for the rolls may begin while the rice is cooking.

2. Add a tiny amount of oil to a medium-sized pan and let it heat up. Each sausage should be seared on both sides in hot oil. Each side should take no more than a minute to complete. Add the garlic after approximately a minute. The sausages should be coated with a little bit of Louisiana spicy sauce. Remove the food from the pan and keep it away for later.

3. Add a little extra oil to the pan and allow it to cook up on a medium-high heat. Add the red and green bell peppers and celery, cut into thin strips. Season with creole spice and cook for approximately a minute on medium-low heat before serving. Set the sausages aside.

4. Wrap a bamboo mat with plastic wrap and secure it. Center a nori sheet on top. Using your hands dampened with water, spread 1 cup of the cooked rice over the seaweed, leaving a quarter-inch border on both sides. Intensify the pressure. Turn the sushi layer over so that the seaweed is facing up and the rice is facing down, keeping the plastic wrap in place on the mat.

5. Assemble your ingredients so that they create a clean row along the nori square nearest to you. 5 Place one sausage strip and one crab log on top of the seaweed. Roll the bamboo mat forward, pushing the contents into the cylinder-shaped sushi, making sure the plastic wrap is still attached to the mat. To form the sushi, use both hands to firmly press the bamboo mat. Make three additional rolls using the remaining ingredients.

6. Use a wet serrated knife to slice the sushi rolls into 1-inch rounds, then whip the slices together. Japanese Creole Sauce with wasabi and ginger is a great accompaniment.

Creole Sauce from Japan

1. Mix mayonnaise, Sriracha Jerk Marinade, and lime juice in a small bowl. To adjust the level of heat, try a little Sriracha and then a little more. You can either serve it right away or preserve it in the fridge for up to a month.

46.SMOKED SALMON & AVOCADO SUSHI

Prep Time: 20 minute | **Cook Time:** 10 minute | **Serves:** 32

INGREDIENTS

- ❖ 300g sushi rice
- ❖ 2 tbsp rice or white wine vinegar
- ❖ 1 tsp caster sugar
- ❖ 1 large avocado
- ❖ juice ½ lemon
- ❖ 4 sheets nori seaweed
- ❖ 4 large slices smoked salmon
- ❖ 1 bunch chives
- ❖ sweet soy sauce (kecap manis), to serve

METHOD

1. Add 600ml of water to a small saucepan and bring it to a boil. Boil for 10 minutes or until the water has been absorbed and the rice has been cooked through. Cover and allow to cool after adding the vinegar and sugar.

2. Remove the avocado's skin, stone, and rind. The lemon juice should be squeezed over the avocado, and

the avocado should be turned so that all the pieces are coated.

3. Make sure to leave a 1cm border on either side of the nori sheets when distributing the rice. Place the salmon on top of the rice, then the chives, and lastly the avocado in the middle.

4. When you're finished, you'll have a tightly rolled seaweed wrap. To aid in the sealing of the roll, lightly wet the top border. Repeat this process four more times. Wrap each roll in cling film and store in the refrigerator until ready to serve.

5. A serrated knife can be used here to cut each roll into eight equal halves. The sweet soy sauce may be used to dip the food in.

47.SALMON & CUCUMBER SUSHI ROLLS

Prep Time: 20 minutes | **Cook Time:** 20 minutes | **Serves:** 12

INGREDIENTS

- ❖ 2 nori sheets
- ❖ 100g skinless salmon fillet (use really fresh), thinly sliced lengthways
- ❖ ¼ cucumber , deseeded, thinly sliced lengthways
- ❖ squeeze wasabi , plus extra to serve
- ❖ pickled sushi ginger , to serve
- ❖ light soy sauce , to serve
- ❖ salmon roe , to serve (optional)
- ❖ For the rice
- ❖ 100g sushi rice
- ❖ 2 tsp saké or mirin (optional)
- ❖ 1 tbsp caster sugar (omit if using mirin)
- ❖ 25ml rice vinegar

METHOD

1. Make the rice first. Using a colander and your hands, rinse the sushi rice until it is completely clear. Allow 15 minutes of draining time.
2. Add 200ml of water and the sake or mirin, if using, to a pot and bring to a boil. To begin, bring the water to a boil, then lower the heat and simmer for 20 minutes until the water has been absorbed. Withdraw from the heat. Cover and let sit for 15-20 minutes.
3. Toss everything into a large bowl and mix. Pour the vinegar and a generous amount of salt over the rice and stir to combine. If using, dissolve the sugar in the

vinegar mixture. Set away at room temperature with a moist tea towel until ready to use.

4. Place a nori sheet on a bamboo mat and spread half of the cooled rice on top of the nori. With the salmon and cucumber pieces, you should be careful not to overfill the rice. Add some wasabi to the edge of the filling by running your finger over it with a pea-sized dab.

5. When you've reached the other end, squeeze to close the roll. Add extra wasabi and additional nori, salmon, and cucumber to your liking. Serve with more wasabi, ginger, soy sauce, and salmon roe, if desired, after slicing each roll into six pieces. One day in the fridge is all that is needed to keep it fresh.

48.SALMON SKIN ROLL

Total Time: 40 mins | **Servings:** 4

INGREDIENTS

- ❖ For the Sushi Rice 1 cup(s)
- ❖ Sushi rice, rinsed 1 1/2 cup(s)
- ❖ Water 1/4 cup(s)
- ❖ Rice vinegar 2 tblsp
- ❖ Sugar 1/4 tsp
- ❖ Salt 1 tsp
- ❖ Sesame oil
- ❖ For the Salmon 300 g
- ❖ Salmon filet, skin-on 1 tblsp
- ❖ Vegetable oil 2 oz
- ❖ Cream cheese, softened 2 tblsp
- ❖ Japanese mayonnaise 1/4 cup(s)
- ❖ Chopped spring onions

- ❖ Salt, to taste
- ❖ For the Rolls 4
- ❖ Sheets nori 1 tsp
- ❖ Togarashi spice 1
- ❖ Small cucumber, peeled and cut into strips
- ❖ Toasted sesame seeds, for rolling
- ❖ Soy sauce and wasabi, for serving

DIRECTIONS

1. Sushi rice must be made beforehand. In a small saucepan, combine the rice with the water. Cook over medium-low heat until the sauce has thickened somewhat, about 10 minutes. Cook for 20 minutes with the lid on. Leave the lid on for a further ten minutes after the heat has been turned off. Sesame oil and sesame vinegar should be heated until the sugar is completely dissolved in the vinegar. Toss the cooked rice with the vinegar mixture and fluff it up with a fork while doing so. Cool the sushi rice once it has been made.

2. After that, you'll need to get the salmon ready. In a non-stick skillet, heat up a tablespoon of vegetable oil and season the salmon with a pinch of salt. Lay the salmon skin-side down on a cutting board or counter. Cook for a further 3 to 5 minutes, or until the skin is crisp and golden. Excess oil may be drained from the salmon by placing it on paper towels.

3. Salmon may be flaked once it has cooled sufficiently to handle. The skin should be saved for another time. In a bowl, combine the cream cheese and mayonnaise and stir until well combined.. Sliced spring onions and flaked salmon should be added.

4. Roll out the dough and put it in the oven. Make sure you have a sushi mat like Helen's Asian Kitchen Bamboo Sushi Rolling Mat on hand before you begin rolling out your sushi. On top of the nori, evenly distribute 34 cup sushi rice. Flip the rice over onto a sheet of wax paper.
5. The next step is to place cucumber strips along the nori's edge. The salmon and cream cheese combination should be placed next to the cucumber.
6. Lift one end of the rolling mat and roll it up to the other end, tying the two ends together. To finish, add in the other ingredients.
7. Using a rolling pin, coat the salmon skin roll with toasted sesame seeds.
8. Chop the salmon skin you saved and combine it with the togarashi in a large dish.
9. Slice each sushi roll into six pieces and place them on a serving tray. Serve with soy sauce and wasabi paste on the side for dipping. Enjoy!

49.SALMON SUSHI ROLLS

Prep Time: 1h 50 mins | **Cook Time:** 20 mins | **Servings:** 4

INGREDIENTS

- ❖ 1 cup sushi rice, rinsed
- ❖ 1 tbsp seasoned rice vinegar
- ❖ 4 nori sheets (dried, roasted seaweed)
- ❖ 1/2 avocado, sliced lengthways
- ❖ 105g can red salmon, drained, flaked
- ❖ 1/2 Lebanese cucumber, cut into thin strips
- ❖ 1 small carrot, grated
- ❖ soy sauce, to serve

METHOD STEPS

1. Over high heat, combine 1 1/2 cups of cold water with 1 cup of rice. Cover and cook for only a few minutes after reaching a boil. Cook for 15 minutes at low heat, or until the rice is cooked and the liquid has been absorbed. Removing the pan from the heat is the right thing to do. Stand for five minutes.

2. In a bowl, combine rice and vinegar. Mix thoroughly. Stirring often will help keep the rice from getting gloppy as it cools.

3. Place a nori sheet on a sushi mat with the glossy side down. Spread one-quarter of the rice mixture over the nori sheet, leaving a 3-inch border around the sides. Place a quarter of the avocado on the edge that is facing you. A quarter of each of the salmon, cucumber, and carrots should be placed on top. Roll tightly to envelop the filling in the sushi mat. Continue with the remaining nori, rice mixture, fish, and veggies.

4. Do this by cutting each roll into four equal pieces. Plastic wrap should be used to protect the food.

50.VOLCANO ROLL

Prep Time: 20 Minutes | **Total Time:** 40 Minutes | **Servings:** 2 Rolls

INGREDIENTS

FOR THE ROLLS:

- ❖ 1 cup cooked sushi rice
- ❖ 1-2 tsp seasoned rice vinegar
- ❖ 2 nori seaweed sheets
- ❖ 4-6 green onion stalks plus extra to garnish
- ❖ 1/4 English cucumber, peeled and sliced or about 1/3 of a regular cucumber
- ❖ 2 TBSP cream cheese optional
- ❖ 1 TBSP of toasted sesame seeds optional

VOLCANO TOPPING: CHOOSE 1

- ❖ 8 jumbo shrimp (raw, defrosted, and cleaned/deveined)
- ❖ 4 ounces raw salmon
- ❖ 4 ounces raw bay scallops or sea scallops

SPICY VOLCANO SAUCE:

- ❖ 2/3 cup quality mayo
- ❖ 2 tablespoons Sriracha
- ❖ whisk togethor and adjust spice/heat as needed

TOOLS NEEDED:

- ❖ bamboo sushi mat to roll the sushi
- ❖ saran/plastic wrap to protect the mat from sticky rice
- ❖ aluminum foil or parchment paper for the seafood
- ❖ a spoon or fork to spread the rice

INSTRUCTIONS

1. 350 degrees Fahrenheit is the ideal temperature for baking.
2. Sushi rice should be cooked and allowed to rest for 10 minutes under a lid. Add seasoned rice vinegar to the skillet and heat through. Allow to cool before fluffing with a fork.
3. At this point, I like to begin making the spicy volcano topping.
4. Toss your raw shrimp, scallops, or salmon (or a mix of the three!) with volcano sauce and serve.
5. Make sure to roll up the aluminum foil around the mixture to keep it from spilling.
6. Bake for 15 minutes, or until the seafood is opaque and cooked through, until the dish is ready to serve. This won't take very long, even if the oven timings differ a little from one batch to another. I recommend sauteing the shrimp on the stovetop until it's almost done, then putting it in the oven with the sauce to finish it off. This is a huge time saver!
7. Lining bamboo mat with plastic wrap and a nori sheet while seafood is baking can help keep your fish fresher for longer.
8. You'll need to slice cucumber into thin strips, lay out two thin strips of cream cheese, and cut up some green onion for this recipe.

9. With your fingers or a spoon, spread a thin layer of rice over the seaweed sheet. Then, in three rows at the far end of the square, arrange your cucumber, cream cheese, and green onion over the rice. Because you'll be making two rolls, divide the toppings evenly between them. You've never rolled sushi before. For a step-by-step pictorial instruction, [click here].
10. Slice, roll, then sprinkle sesame seeds on top of the rolls!
11. Finally, your bright orange volcanic topping is done. If you'd like, you may top the seafood with a little extra sauce and broil it for a few seconds. Since this is the closest I can get to the golden topping served at my local sushi restaurant, I like making it. If you don't want to use the excess sauce, you may just leave it out. Add a few more sprigs of minced green onion to the volcano topping before pouring it over your cucumber roll.

51.SHRIMP TEMPURA ROLL

Prep Time: 25 Minutes | **Total Time:** 40 Minutes | **Servings:** 4 Rolls

INGREDIENTS

For the sushi rice:

- ❖ 2 cups uncooked sushi rice
- ❖ 2 cups water
- ❖ 2 tablespoons rice vinegar
- ❖ 2 tablespoons sugar
- ❖ 1 1/2 teaspoons salt

For the sushi rolls:

- ❖ 4 sheets of nori
- ❖ 8 pre-cooked tempura shrimp
- ❖ 8 strips of cucumber
- ❖ 8 slices of avocado
- ❖ 3 tablespoons black and/or white sesame seeds

INSTRUCTIONS

1. In a colander, rinse the rice until the water becomes clear.
2. Add 2 cups of water and the rice to a medium pot and bring to a boil. Cover and bring to a boil over medium-high heat, stirring occasionally. The heat should be reduced to low and the lid should be put on after it reaches a boil. 15 minutes of cooking time. To cool the pot entirely, cover it with a lid for 10 minutes and then remove it from the heat source.
3. In a small dish, combine rice vinegar, sugar, and salt; microwave for 20-30 seconds until warm. Add the vinegar mixture to the rice in a large bowl. When

you're done kneading, you'll be Allow the rice to cool to room temperature.

4. Place one nori sheet on a flat surface and press 1/3-1/2 cup rice all the way over the nori's surface. It's easier to do this with somewhat moist fingertips.

5. Invert a sushi mat so that the seaweed side is up and place a piece of plastic wrap over the rice-covered nori.

6. Along one side of the nori, arrange 2 shrimp, 2 cucumber strips, and 2 avocado slices.

7. Roll the sushi tightly starting with the edge of the mat closest to the shrimp mixture and working your way outward.

8. Sesame seeds, about 2 tablespoons, should be pressed into the sushi rice.

9. Slice the sushi and serve it right away with a sharp knife.

52.SNOW SUSHI ROLL

Prep Time: 20 minutes | **Servings:** 2 rolls

INGREDIENTS

- ❖ 8 sticks imitation crab
- ❖ 1 mini cucumber
- ❖ 1 Tbsp mayonnaise
- ❖ 1 Tbsp lemon juice
- ❖ 4 drops sriracha or up to spice tolerant
- ❖ 1½ cup cooked sushi rice
- ❖ 3 Tbsp sushi vinegar
- ❖ 2 sheet nori use ¾ of each sheet
- ❖ 1 tsp roasted sesame seeds optional for garnishing

INSTRUCTIONS

1. Slice a cucumber into matchstick-sized pieces.
2. Slice up a jar of imitation crab into pieces.
3. Add a few drops of sriracha or your preferred spicy sauce to the mayonnaise, lemon juice, and salt. Be sure to thoroughly combine the ingredients.
4. Ten to twenty minutes in the fridge is enough time for the mixture to cool.
5. Sushi vinegar OR rice/apple vinegar with 14 tsp. sugar and 14 tsp. salt can be used to season sushi rice.
6. Place your bamboo mat on a level surface covered in plastic wrapping.
7. Another piece of plastic wrap should be placed on top of the bamboo mat.
8. Lay a plastic/bamboo mat on top of a 34-torn sheet of nori.

9. Flip the entire sheet over so that the nori side is facing up and spread rice over the top.
10. Place the crab salad on top and garnish with pieces of cucumber.
11. To make a uramaki sushi roll, just lift, tuck, and roll the ingredients together.
12. On one end of the plastic wrapping, spread a layer of crab salad.
13. Finally, top it all off with a sushi roll!
14. This time, the crab salad will cover the sushi roll's top, giving a beautiful marbled snow appearance. Carefully roll again.
15. Slice into small pieces for easy consumption.
16. After unwrapping the sesame seeds, sprinkle them on top of the dish.
1. Serve immediately, or refrigerate for a few minutes for a refreshing taste.

53.SOFT SHELL CRAB SUSHI ROLL

Cook Time: 18 mins | **Total Time:** 38 mins | **Servings:** 4

INGREDIENTS

- ❖ 8 soft shell crabs
- ❖ 2-3 avocados cut into long strips
- ❖ 2-3 small cucumbers peeled and cut into matchsticks
- ❖ 1 package alfalfa sprouts cut into smaller segments
- ❖ 8 seaweed sheets
- ❖ 1 egg yolk lightly beaten
- ❖ 1 cup iced water
- ❖ 1/2 cup gluten free flour plus more for coating
- ❖ 1/2 cup cornstarch
- ❖ 1/2 teaspoon baking powder
- ❖ ice water bath (fill larger bowl than the one that will be used for the batter with ice and some water)
- ❖ oil for deep frying
- ❖ gluten free tamari wasabi (optional) and spicy mayo (optional) for serving

INSTRUCTIONS

1. In a big dish, add ice water. Stir in the beaten egg yolk gradually, using chopsticks, into the icy water. Stir in the flour, cornstarch, and baking powder with a fork until just mixed, then add the other ingredients. Ideally, the batter will be lumpy and runny. Keep the batter in an ice bath during frying by putting it in a bigger ice bath basin.
2. To cook fish, heat a small saucepan of oil to 340 degrees Fahrenheit over medium/medium-high heat. Testing the temperature of the oil may be done without a thermometer by dropping a little batter into

the heated oil and watching it rise to the top. The soft shell crab should be thoroughly immersed in oil.

3. First coat the soft shell crabs with flour, then put them into a heated oil. 3-4 minutes on each side, depending on the size of your pot; turn them over in the middle of the cooking process. Drain on paper towels after removing from oil. Repeat for the remaining soft-shell crabs.

4. Using a seaweed sheet in front of you, arrange an avocado, cucumber, alfalfa and soft shell crab half on the lowest third of the sheet. Roll away from you, being sure to keep everything in place while you do so. Use a sharp knife to cut into six equal pieces. Please repeat this process for all other components.

5. The seaweed sheet is placed on top, the contents are layered and the roll is securely held together before being rolled away from you if you have a bamboo sushi rolling mat.

6. Garnish with spicy mayo and gluten-free tamari (mixture of mayo and Sriracha)

THE END

Printed in Great Britain
by Amazon

16770422R00063